Understanding Nonverbal
Learning Disabilities

Understanding Nonverbal Learning Disabilities

A Common-Sense Guide for Parents and Professionals

Maggie Mamen

Jessica Kingsley Publishers
London and Philadelphia

First published in 2007
by Jessica Kingsley Publishers
116 Pentonville Road
London N1 9JB, UK
and
400 Market Street, Suite 400
Philadelphia, PA 19106, USA

www.jkp.com

Some of the content was previously published as: *Nonverbal Learning Disabilities and Their Clinical Subtypes: Assessment, Diagnosis and Management* First Edition: September 2000, Second Edition: October 2000, Third Edition: July 2001, Fourth Edition: November 2002, and as *Nonverbal Learning Disabilities and Their Clinical Subtypes: A Handbook for Parents and Professionals – New Edition* March 2006

Library of Congress Cataloging in Publication Data
Mamen, Maggie, 1946-
    Understanding nonverbal learning disabilities : a common-sense guide for parents and professionals / Maggie Mamen. -- 1st American pbk. ed.
        p. cm. -- (JKP essentials)
    Includes bibliographical references.
    ISBN-13: 978-1-84310-593-0 (pb : alk. paper) 1. Nonverbal learning disabilities. I. Title.
    RJ506.L4M36 2007
    618.92'85889--dc22

                                                    2007007800

British Library Cataloguing in Publication Data
A CIP catalogue record for this book is available from the British Library

ISBN 978 1 84310 593 0

Printed and bound in the United States by
Thomas-Shore, Inc.

CONTENTS

List of tables

OVERVIEW

This guide started out several years ago as the notes for presentations and handouts to groups of parents, educators, and other professionals, and grew through five previous drafts. Its metamorphosis is primarily due to the ongoing discussions and consultations shared with professionals and parents from all over the province of Ontario, and across provincial and national borders. In addition, hundreds of children, adolescents and adults have provided invaluable data, observations, and experiences of nonverbal learning difficulties (NLDs) in all their forms. Feedback from parents, teachers, and other professionals has been both encouraging and thought-provoking, and has continued to produce new questions, to generate new hypotheses, and to provide new ideas.

This classification of subtypes of NLD is founded on clinical practice – those individuals we see in our offices for assessments and interventions – not on empirically based research studies. In our multidisciplinary practice, our experiences with clients of all ages tell us repeatedly that not all individuals with NLD show the full range of difficulties that are contained in the literature on the NLD syndromes. For example, while many have noticeable social difficulties or problems with balance and coordination, still others are socially popular and athletically talented. We have thus concluded that grouping all individuals with NLD under one diagnostic "label," especially when attempting to generate a useful set of recommendations, is neither realistic nor helpful, since there appear to be as many differences within the group as there are between this group and other learning exceptionalities. In addition, the sheer volume of symptoms, behaviors, emotional factors, and other issues presented by such eminent authors as Byron Rourke, Sue Thompson, and others are more often than not completely overwhelming and distressing for those people involved in any aspect of NLD from either a personal or a professional perspective. Thus, it is our belief that separating the major presenting issues into four clusters, or "subtypes," can be helpful in understanding, assessing, diagnosing, and managing individuals with learning disabilities by giving everyone a focus and a place to start.

The purpose of this guide is not simply to review and update the original information several years down the road from its inception, but also to introduce the concept of pattern recognition deficits as being fundamental to a range of difficulties experienced by individuals with NLD. As with the idea of clinical subtypes, the role of pattern recognition in NLD, while a common-sense connection to make in terms of learning clearly being the recognition and reproduction of some kind of pattern, is not grounded in systematic research. Rather, it emerges as an intriguing idea that provides not only a paradigm for understanding many of the diverse presenting symptoms that constitute this complex disorder, but also a framework for suggesting some common-sense strategies that open up more possibilities for remediation and compensation.

There are many factors that impact a person's ability to learn. These factors include both intrinsic and extrinsic issues, including genetics, motivation, level of environmental stimulation, language of instruction, family crises, chaotic and/or dysfunctional family situation, separation and divorce, physical or mental illness, problems with hearing or vision, inadequate instructional opportunities, and so on. It is not the purpose of this guide to explore any of these – simply to ensure that there is an awareness that an NLD is only one of a number of factors that should be considered in the presence of learning difficulties.

Thanks to my colleagues at Centrepointe Professional Services (in particular, Dr. Joel Kanigsberg, Dr. Jody Alberts-Corush, Dr. Susan Rich, Dr. James Lazowski, Dr. Carrie Horne, Dr. Petra Duschner, Meg Waurick, Judi Laurikainen, and Sally Lees); there have been many spirited and inspiring discussions by the photocopier, over coffee or at brown-bag lunches with respect to the various clients who fill our caseloads. Brenda Case, our educational consultant, is a goldmine of ideas when it comes to teaching strategies and I am particularly grateful to her for a number of the suggestions for teachers contained in this guide. She is also unflaggingly willing to help children with various learning problems through her diagnostic teaching, tutoring, and training activities. We are all seeing more and more children who present with nonverbal deficits, and yearn to take time out of our busy practices to conduct some research on the ideas and hypotheses that our experiences continue to generate. The sections on Developmental Coordination Disorder were contributed by Dr Cheryl Missiuna, Ph.D and O.T. Reg (Ont.) who is an occupational therapist (OT) at the school of Rehabilitation Science at McMaster University in Hamilton, Ontario, and head of CanChild, and Denise DeLaat, also an OT, from the Children's Hospital of Eastern Ontario in

Ottawa. Their contributions are much appreciated, and serve to emphasize the need for a multidisciplinary perspective in the field of NLD.

The major purpose of our involvement with individuals with NLD is to help them, their parents and educators, and others who live and work with this complex learning problem, to understand what is going on, where their strengths and weaknesses lie, how to predict challenging situations, and what can be done to assist these youngsters. It is with these goals in mind that the guide has been written. While the focus is on children, much of it also holds true for individuals of all ages. It is not meant to be exhaustive, but is intended to act as a "seed" paper to generate further debate and, it is hoped, some research-based verification of the notion of subtypes of NLD. At the same time, it includes a number of general suggestions that have proved to be helpful in terms of addressing the needs of the various subtypes that we are proposing. These strategies are presented in terms of the particular need, rather than by subtype, since there is quite definitely some overlap for many children and since there is usually one particular issue that takes precedence over others at any given time.

Alas, none of the strategies or suggestions comes with a money-back guarantee, and the efficacy of any single one will depend heavily on factors such as motivation, drive, personality, parent–child relationships, teacher variables, behavioral issues, and everything else that contributes to our inter- and intrapersonal environments. Common-sense and intuition are invaluable, however, and nothing ventured is always nothing gained. As Henry Ford reportedly said: "Whether you think you can, or whether you think you cannot, you are right!" (www.landofwisdom.com/author/henry-ford/page6.html).

I should like to acknowledge a very special debt of gratitude to the many parents and clients who have shared their very personal, insightful, and sometimes quite distressing experiences with me. In particular, a very dynamic lady from Kitchener-Waterloo, Cheryl Pidgeon, a co-founder of NLD Ontario, a network of enthusiastic and committed parents, has been an inspiration, a strong supporter, and a source of endless questions and challenges. It is interactions such as these that keep this project alive and dynamic.

Chapter 1

INTRODUCTION TO LEARNING DISABILITIES

Definition

While there have been many and varying attempts at definition since learning disabilities were first identified in the 1960s, the general consensus is that a learning disability (LD) is the result of some disruption in the psychological processes basic to effective learning, in the context of at least average general cognitive functioning in key areas of thinking and reasoning. For example, the following definition was endorsed by the Learning Disabilities Association of Canada in 2002, following a task force report from the Learning Disabilities Association of Ontario in 2001:

> "Learning Disabilities" refer to a number of disorders which may affect the acquisition, organization, retention, understanding or use of verbal or nonverbal information. These disorders affect learning in individuals who otherwise demonstrate at least average abilities essential for thinking and/or reasoning. As such, learning disabilities are distinct from global intellectual deficiency.
>
> Learning disabilities result from impairments in one or more processes related to perceiving, thinking, remembering or learning. These include, but are not limited to: language processing; phonological processing; visual spatial processing; processing speed; memory and attention; and executive functions (e.g. planning and decision-making).
>
> Learning disabilities range in severity and may interfere with the acquisition and use of one or more of the following: oral language (e.g. listening, speaking, understanding); reading (e.g. decoding, phonetic knowledge, word recognition, comprehension); written language (e.g.

spelling and written expression); and mathematics (e.g. computation, problem-solving).

Learning disabilities may also involve difficulties with organizational skills, social perception, social interaction and perspective taking.

Learning disabilities are lifelong. The way in which they are expressed may vary over an individual's lifetime, depending on the interaction between the demands of the environment and the individual's strengths and needs. Learning disabilities are suggested by unexpected academic under-achievement or achievement which is maintained only by unusually high levels of effort and support.

Learning disabilities are due to genetic and/or neurobiological factors or injury that alters brain functioning in a manner which affects one or more processes related to learning. These disorders are not due primarily to hearing and/or vision problems, socio-economic factors, cultural or linguistic differences, lack of motivation or ineffective teaching, although these factors may further complicate the challenges faced by individuals with learning disabilities. Learning disabilities may co-exist with various conditions including attentional, behavioral and emotional disorders, sensory impairments or other medical conditions.

For success, individuals with learning disabilities require early identification and timely specialized assessments and interventions involving home, school, community and workplace settings. The interventions need to be appropriate for each individual's learning disability subtype and, at a minimum, include the provision of: specific skill instruction; accommodations; compensatory strategies; self-advocacy skills.

The general definition itself is applicable to all types of learning disabilities, and does not differentiate those which are primarily language-based (LLD) from those that are the result of difficulties with the processing of nonverbal information (NLD), or those whose problems lie primarily in the area of executive functioning. It is, however, generally understood that individuals with LLD show deficits in language-based and language-related psychological processes, such as auditory processing, vocabulary acquisition, syntax, etc., whereas individuals with NLD are more likely to show deficits in nonverbal psychological processes such as visual, spatial, and/or motor functioning.

Making the "learning cake"

In order to help understand the concept of learning disabilities, an analogy provides more familiar terms.

Ingredients

Learning can be seen as being like baking a cake. All cakes have a basic set of *ingredients*; so does learning. Almost all cakes have a basis of flour, and some binding ingredient(s), such as eggs, butter, margarine, oil, water, juice, apple sauce, etc. These are the average levels of *thinking and reasoning skills* that constitute the basis of definitions of learning situations. The more we have, the bigger the cake we can make. The less we have, the

smaller or less adequate that cake may be. Similarly, if we are well-endowed with a range of thinking and reasoning skills, the stronger the foundation will be to support a range of learning tasks. On top of these basic components, each different type of cake requires a variety of additional ingredients, the unique combination of which is responsible for the almost infinite variety of finished products. If any of these ingredients are unavailable or available but omitted, the cake will not turn out as planned – and may even fail completely, depending upon the significance of that particular ingredient for the flavor and cooking process. It may be possible to substitute some similar ingredient(s) that may work as well, or almost as well. We can replace sugar with aspartame, butter with apple sauce, almonds with walnuts – the cake may look or taste different, and we may or may not notice this difference. When it comes to learning, we may be able to substitute a visual approach to a reading task, if a child is lacking good auditory skills, for example. We may be able to memorize something we cannot reason through, or we may be able to work out something we cannot memorize. We may be able to *talk aloud* in order to translate visual material into words so that we can substitute our verbal reasoning for a lack of visual-spatial reasoning skills. Just like the cakes, sometimes, the finished product will be fairly similar to what was required; some-times, it will not. Either way, it will probably take longer to complete, require higher levels of energy and more sustained motivation, and be far more frustrating or anxiety-provoking, and much less satisfying to the "cook."

Proportions

In addition to having all the ingredients, or suitable substitutes where available, it is important to have the ingredients in the correct *proportions*. If a child has 25 kg of flour, but no eggs, the cake will flop – badly. Giving the child more and more flour and encouraging him or her to use it will not make the cake turn out any better. In fact, the balance of ingredients will become worse, and people may become even more impatient when the cake is still not successful, despite much effort. Parents and teachers alike are puzzled when a child who seems to be very gifted verbally, and whose remaining skills are still within the average range for his or her age, simply cannot learn well. For NLD children, it is the frequently more subtle nonverbal ingredients that are insufficient; for LLD children, it is the sometimes more obvious language-based ones. If we work exclusively to increase an NLD child's verbal abilities, without making sure that they are associated and blended with the nonverbal aspects of learning, we may see little or no measurable improvement.

Recipe

We may have all the ingredients in the world available to us, or we may have found adequate substitutes, but we still may be stuck unless we follow the *recipe*, without which we do not know which of the ingredients to use, in what proportion, in what order we need to combine them, and what we are supposed to do with them. In other words, there may well be a problem with the *process* of learning, and not with the availability of appropriate tools. The majority of us pick up the process of learning simply by repeated exposure, practice, and eventual internalization of the *rules* by which we acquire information, interact with others, and figure out situations, be they math problems or establishing friendships. We recognize and follow unspoken routines, and can maintain interpersonal interactions by *knowing* what we are likely to need to do or say next. The process of learning involves recognizing a pattern, perceiving the various parts that make up that pattern, and seeing how they fit together to make the *whole*.

Ending up with the right cake, or mastering the particular learning task, is arguably the most important outcome. However, the experience of the process can be what makes a difference to an individual's sense of competence, self-esteem, and even quality of life. When we assess a particular child, individual skills may well be present, perhaps even in reasonably adequate proportions, and we may not always see the huge discrepancies between aptitude and achievement, or among the different aptitudes, that are commonly anticipated in children with learning disabilities. Watching these children perform, their difficulties with the "recipe" are glaringly obvious as we see them struggle with day-to-day tasks and routines.

We can sometimes *measure* and hence quantify an individual's ability to attend, remember, plan, monitor, and organize his or her experiences so that we can legitimately compare his or her performance with that of another individual of the same age, gender, and sometimes even ethnicity. We can also ask others to comment on and rate how a specific child thinks, reasons, and solves problems in order to effect similar comparisons. Children, especially prior to puberty, are only just beginning to develop the cognitive structures that enable them to do this type of introspection to comment for themselves, although it is always wise to ask because we often learn much from the child's own perspective. However, even some of us never develop the capability to analyze or evaluate *how* or *why* we do what we do as we think, reason and remember; we just do it. It is, therefore, frequently difficult, if not impossible, to measure or quantify the *process* by which someone learns, even though this is a necessary prerequisite to understanding how to help. Thus, experience, anecdotal information, astute observation, comparison with others, and our own reactions to working or living with LD individuals all play a vital part in understanding what is going right and what is going wrong with someone's capability to learn, since focusing only on the ingredients without the recipe will probably not result in a successful cake.

Common issues in individuals with LD

As human beings, we possess an incredibly complex central nervous system that is processing constantly, not only that information bombarding us from outside ourselves via all of our senses simultaneously, but also enormous amounts of information from within ourselves, our brains, our bodies, and our minds. We are the only species endowed with the ability to use symbolic language to communicate some of our inner thoughts, and we have generated almost infinite ways of labeling verbally much of what we process. It is therefore quite difficult, and sometimes impossible, to separate verbal from nonverbal thinking. We may be able to draw, sculpt, mimic, demonstrate, gesticulate, compose music, use facial expressions and body language, and otherwise attempt to communicate what we want others to understand. Nonetheless, almost everything we do has a verbal as well as a nonverbal component. Our brains are not organized such that higher-level processes like understanding and reproducing language, reading, mathematics, written expression, and so on, are likely to be located in one particular place, or that one can be definitively distinguished from the others. Rather, the brain is a constantly changing, highly complex *network* of systems, all of which need to work together if we are to learn efficiently.

While the focus of this guide is clearly on individuals with NLD, there are a number of issues that most, if not all, individuals with learning disabilities have in common. In addition, there are many individuals whose learning disabilities cannot be attributed specifically to either language-based problems or nonverbal deficits. For example, some individuals may show generalized sequencing difficulties in all sensory channels or *modalities* (visual, auditory, motor), or generalized short-term memory problems, no matter which input channel is used for information processing. Similarly, there are some people for whom problems with attention and concentration disrupt their learning, regardless of the type of task in which they are engaging. Most have problems with what is called *executive functioning*, which includes the abilities to plan, organize, and monitor our own thinking and activities.

It is not necessary, or arguably even advisable, always to seek to fit an individual precisely into a "type" or "subtype," although it is a fundamental assumption of this guide that some kind of clustering, or subtyping, can definitely be very useful. Rather, it is more important to analyze the learning task requirements in order to identify required skills and abilities, and then to explore an individual's unique profile of strengths and weaknesses in order to predict the kinds of difficulties that are likely to be encountered, and to identify areas for potential remediation and compensation. This said, we can proceed to investigate the common clusters of abilities that underlie different patterns of academic and social learning.

Language-based learning disabilities (LLD)

For a child to be diagnosed with a language-based learning disability, his or her thinking and reasoning skills must be within the broad average range, with deficits in at least one major aspect of linguistic processing that can be directly related to his or her learning problems. For children with auditory and/or language processing problems, it is quite likely to be nonverbal reasoning skills (e.g. pattern recognition, analysis/synthesis, visual concept formation, part–whole concepts, etc.) that are assessed as being strengths. However, some children with LLD do well on verbal reasoning tasks, such as tests where leeway is given for imprecise expressive language. For example, a child who is asked to explain how a firefighter and a police officer are alike might say: "Him wear clothes like each other. Get him out of cars because they crash." This would result in credit being given for a correct response on a verbal reasoning subtest, but yet would clearly indicate that the child had language difficulties. Deficits in linguistic/auditory processing could include problems with discrimination of sounds, short-term or long-term auditory memory, central auditory processing, sequencing of sounds, development of ideas, receptive and/or expressive vocabulary, syntax, semantics, listening comprehension, sound/symbol correspondence, phonological awareness, and so on.

Difficulties in primary language processing (such as auditory discrimination of linguistically meaningful sounds, blending of sounds into words, understanding and development of vocabulary and syntax, comprehension of verbally presented information, organizing linguistic output, and so on) are most often associated with learning problems in the acquisition of secondary language skills, most notably reading and other language-based arts. It is, of course, important to remember that mathematics has a complex "language" of its own. There are children who may have an excellent grasp of such concepts as quantity, sets, time, space, measurement, but who do not understand that "minus," "take away," "less than," "gives one to," etc., are synonymous and represent a particular mathematical operation.

Students whose auditory and/or linguistic processes interfere with their learning are traditionally labeled as learning disabled (LD) or language learning disabled (LLD), and various remedial approaches have been available for these children for some time. The services of speech-language pathologists are invaluable for assessment, therapy, and consultation with respect to learning needs and teaching strategies.

Differences between LLD and NLD

Table 1.1 outlines some of the major differences between LLD and NLD. Social and behavioral difficulties are frequently found in children with any type of learning problem, primarily because appropriate social behavior needs to be learned, just as any academic subject needs to be learned, and thus is likely to be disrupted by the same processing deficits that interfere with other aspects of the child's learning environment.

Mild intellectual disabilities and developmental delay

Children whose abilities essential to thinking and reasoning are assessed to be *globally* below average, and whose cognitive-developmental milestones are lagging behind their peers, are classified as either mildly intellectually disabled (MID) or developmentally disabled (DD), depending upon the degree of impairment. They tend to have difficulties in all academic areas. Appropriate interventions are generally slower paced, developmentally based, and geared to the acquisition of basic literacy and numeracy, as well as adaptive behavioral, communication, and life skills.

Table 1.1 Summary of the major differences between LLD and NLD

Language learning disabilities	Nonverbal learning disabilities
Frequently show strengths in most or all	
• nonverbal thinking and reasoning abilities	• vocabulary development
• visual pattern recognition	• general knowledge
• analysis/synthesis of spatial information	• oral presentation, verbal fluency
• visual concept formation	• auditory attention
• nonverbal part–whole concepts	• sound discrimination
• spatial reasoning	• short-term auditory memory
• short-term and long-term visual memory	• long-term auditory memory
• visual-motor integration	• sequencing of sounds
• fine motor skills	• syntax, grammar
• visual perception	• listening comprehension
• tactile perception	• phonological awareness
Commonly present with weaknesses in one or more	
• receptive and/or expressive vocabulary	• nonverbal thinking and reasoning abilities
• auditory attention	• pattern recognition and reproduction
• sound discrimination	• visual concept formation
• short-term auditory memory	• part–whole concepts
• long-term auditory memory	• analysis of complex tasks into component parts
• central auditory processing	• spatial reasoning, directionality
• sequencing of sounds	• concepts of time, space, distance, speed
• organization of ideas in words	• short-term and long-term visual memory
• syntax	• visual-motor integration
• semantics	• motor planning and fine motor skills
• listening comprehension	• visual perception, tactile perception
• phonological awareness	

Table 1.1 continued

Language learning disabilities	Nonverbal learning disabilities
Generally leading to difficulties in the following areas	
• early reading acquisition	• reading comprehension (non-factual)
• sound/symbol correspondence	• mathematical reasoning
• decoding	• math concepts
• phonics	• relationships among numbers
• reading comprehension	• measurement
• written language	• geometry, trigonometry
• composition, sequencing of ideas	• graphs, diagrams
• use of appropriate vocabulary	• maps
• oral presentations	• organizational skills
• oral responses in class	• time management
• mathematics	• project management
• language of math	• management of personal belongings, personal space, boundary issues
• word problems	• social skills
• social skills	• behavior
• behavior	

There is a small subset of children who appear to meet criteria for both MID and LD. These are children whose overall cognitive abilities fall within what is known as the *borderline* range (standard scores of 70–80, where the average range is 90–110), perhaps even showing borderline scores for some of the important subscales, such as composite verbal and/or nonverbal scales of commonly utilized tests of intellectual ability. However, examination of the individual subtests may show high variability, with some measures of thinking and reasoning abilities falling within the broad range of average, including low average. The main issue with these children is that they may require *both* specialized teaching to take advantage of their relative strengths and remediate their specific weaknesses, *as well as* a slower pace of learning and modified academic expectations.

Children within the DD range have measurable intellectual abilities that are weaker than 99 percent of their age peers, placing them at what is known as the 1st percentile. These children require very specific programming, geared to basic survival literacy and adaptive skills. While on occasion they show *splinter* strengths (e.g. in short-term rote memory), it is highly unlikely that any measure of their thinking and reasoning skills falls within even the broad range of average.

Chapter 2

WHAT THE EYE DOESN'T SEE... RECOGNIZING NLD

Background

It has long been accepted that communication skills are substantially nonverbal, some would claim to the tune of 90 percent. It should not, therefore, come as a surprise that disruptions in nonverbal psychological processes can affect a range of learning tasks, perhaps even to a greater, albeit more subtle, extent than disruptions in language-based abilities.

The concept of nonverbal learning disabilities (NLD) has been around for more than three decades, primarily stemming from the work of Dr. Byron Rourke and his colleagues from the University of Windsor in Southern Ontario (e.g. Rourke 1995), who have proposed a "syndrome" of NLD that is broad and encompassing, and is based on primary, secondary, and tertiary deficits in neuropsychological processes. Surprisingly, however, much of the literature deals with adults for whom nonverbal deficits are secondary to certain types of acute brain damage, and NLD as an *educational* phenomenon is still in its infancy, especially with the acceptance of such a differential diagnosis, appropriate identification, funding support, teacher education, and remedial planning. The work of Sue Thompson has been important in providing recognition and a wide range of recommendations for dealing with NLD children in the school system (e.g. Thompson 1997). Further detailed information can be obtained from the following websites: www.nldontario.org, www.nldontheweb.org and www.nldline.com. However, the diagnosis of NLD within the school setting, along with the provision of appropriate modifications and accommodations, is still something of a work in progress.

Rather than *being* nonverbal, individuals with NLD generally present with abundant verbal ability, with many showing precocious language development and high levels of vocabulary and general knowledge. For individuals with NLD, a missing recipe – or knowledge of the appropriate process of learning – is frequently the main issue impeding their progress. Many of them do not even know what cake they are making, let alone what ingredients to use, when to use them, or how to use them. They often depend on others to tell them – which others may do with varying degrees of patience or frustration. This reliance on others may well become entrenched to the point that children, in particular, may develop quite an entourage – parents, teachers, teacher's aide, resource teacher, tutor, study buddy, and so on – to help cue them as to what to do when. As adults, they may rely unduly on a partner or even still a parent, way beyond the time when functional autonomy would normally be expected.

Presenting issues in NLD

Because of their well-developed verbal abilities, good rote memory, and early phonological awareness skills, the reason for referral for individuals who are subsequently diagnosed as NLD often focuses on issues other than academic problems. In general, the initial presenting observations of students with NLD by parents and teachers tend to be some combination of the following:

- behavioral, social and/or emotional concerns, rather than academic
- strengths in verbal areas; often referred for "gifted" assessment, especially in the early years of school
- problems with sensory input (e.g. overly sensitive to textures of food, clothing, loud sounds, bright lights, etc.)
- motor awkwardness, clumsiness, poor coordination
- weaknesses in visual-motor integration and fine motor control
- difficulties with executive functions (planning, monitoring, self-regulation, attention, organizational skills)
- reluctance to change routines once established
- difficulties with part–whole relationships
- problems with organizational skills
- trouble establishing and/or maintaining friendships
- difficulty adjusting conversational level to be appropriate for different listeners

- inability to grasp and manipulate spatial relationships in two and three dimensions
- trouble understanding concepts of time, distance, space, direction
- difficulties recognizing personal space and boundaries.

There are many different circumstances and disorders that may give rise to each of these "symptoms" or even combinations of any or all of them. It is normally not unless, or until, a psychological or psychoeducational assessment is undertaken that the child's cognitive profile reveals a telling profile of nonverbal deficits, pattern recognition difficulties and processing problems that underlie many of the behavioral, social and learning issues experienced in the school environment and beyond. It is therefore critical, if a diagnosis of NLD is to be considered, that a full psychological assessment be conducted, including cognitive testing, behavioral observations, full parent and teacher interviews, visual-motor assessment, social skills screening and some personality assessment. In most cases, a multi-disciplinary assessment is required in order to provide access to the knowledge, experience and skill sets of such professionals as occupational therapists, speech-language pathologists, and educators.

Early identification of NLD

The early identification of NLD, especially in younger children, has traditionally presented some problems. This is primarily because these youngsters quite frequently, if not almost exclusively, present initially with difficulties other than the academic lags traditionally seen in the language learning disabled (LLD) population. Behavior problems, social difficulties, low frustration tolerance, verbal abuse, and poor or nonexistent written work are just some of the presenting issues that bring such children to the attention of psychological or social service providers, particularly in the first few grades. It is not uncommon for there to be few, or even no, worries on the part of teachers regarding academic progress during the primary years. Given the nature of NLD, in that it often affects the *integration* of basic skills, rather than their *acquisition*, academics are not usually significantly affected until the child has been in school for four or five years, at the point where the emphasis in the classroom switches from straightforward skill mastery to the need to choose which skills to use in order to address more complex academics, specifically reading comprehension, math problem-solving and creative writing.

Risk factors in preschool children

While none of the following is a specific or definitive indication of potential NLD problems, and many of them are common in early childhood, the continuing presence of one or more may well be a risk factor requiring at least careful monitoring and possible assessment, especially if they are interfering with the normal course of learning:

- active avoidance of fine motor activities (e.g. coloring, drawing, puzzles, Lego)
- problems with intelligibility or fluency of speech
- difficulties with subtle aspects of language (e.g. humor, analogy, symbolic language)
- poor social use of language
- misinterpretation of visual cues, social cues
- poor social interactions
- hypersensitivity to visual, auditory, tactile stimulation
- problems with gross motor activities (e.g. balance, coordination, left–right confusion)
- eye–hand coordination difficulties.

Children presenting for assessment in later elementary years or beyond often have a prior history of involvement from speech-language services – primarily for articulation, stuttering, or other difficulties with the mechanics or fluency of speech – and/or occupational therapy for assistance with gross and/or fine motor development. Often, this involvement was discontinued because the child appeared to catch up to age-expected levels. However, there are frequently some residual problems that persist and interfere with the acquisition of or fluency with academic skills. For example, a youngster who, as a preschooler, had identified difficulties with motor sequencing activities (e.g. eye–hand coordination, balance, putting on or taking off clothing or shoes, coordinating lip, tongue, and breathing, etc.) may well have problems later on with the acquisition of such skills as handwriting, spelling, and organizing written math.

Verbal abilities

Adding to the confusion is the fact that many NLD children have such strong, sometimes superior or very superior, verbal abilities that they are frequently an enigma to those who live with and teach them, and it is often extremely hard for parents, teachers and others to come to terms with the fact that there may be a learning disability of any kind. Because of their often superior acquisition of vocabulary and general knowledge, and because they are often reported to be bored with the (to them) more difficult coloring, printing, and other fine motor tasks, it is quite common for these children to be referred for assessment for giftedness. It generally comes as quite a blow to parents that there is more to intellectual giftedness than precocious language skills, and that nonverbal abilities, including emotional maturity, are usually required for true learning to take place.

On the somewhat more negative side, verbal strengths may be used both as a defense and as a weapon, and individuals with them are sometimes viewed as "mouthy," overly verbose, or even verbally aggressive. Since expressive vocabulary is usually seen by most people as a reliable predictor of a person's general intelligence, individuals with NLD are frequently expected to perform uniformly as competently as they appear to be from their superficial verbal abilities. They frequently talk their way into many situations for which they do not possess the substantive follow-through, and their facility with words may result in the delegation to them of more responsibility than they are actually able to handle. In relationships, they may often promise much more than they are capable of following through, resulting in disappointment and damaged expectations. Frustration is thus very common, a natural result of the discrepancy between expectation and reality, on the part of not only those with NLD, but also those who live or work with them.

Language difficulties in NLD

Despite the fact that the primary focus of NLD lies, by definition, in nonverbal psychological process deficits, there are a number of language skills that are nonetheless affected. Pattern recognition is critical when processing verbal input – not simply to recognize the sounds of words so that they can be learned, remembered, and linked directly with what they mean, but also to recognize the myriad nonverbal information that helps us understand more than the words. What these patterns include is discussed below.

Tone of voice, loudness, pace

These help us understand the speaker's feelings, intention, mood, and so forth, and may indicate more complex emotional factors, such as degree of intimacy, respect, and other interpersonal information. Most of us have had occasion to say: "It's not *what* you said, it's *how* you said it." While a loud voice may be appropriate for a noisy environment, or outdoors, a lower amplitude is most often appropriate when someone is nearby, when a particular communication is intimate, private or personal, and generally when it is not appropriate for others to hear. When we increase the pace of our speech, we are usually indicating urgency, and frequently intend to communicate a need to hurry. When we slow it down, we are often adjusting to the recipient's level of understanding, or perhaps indicating our own need to think carefully about what we are saying.

Emphasis on a particular word or phrase

We need to know the difference between, for example, "I *want* to come later" and "I want to come *later*," if we are to anticipate someone else's actions and respond appropriately. Individuals with NLD frequently tune in only to the specific words that are being spoken, and may provide their own, sometimes inaccurate, interpretation of intent.

Use of sarcasm, irony, humor, etc.

In social situations, as well as in more academic settings, we need to know when someone means what they are saying, or whether they are teasing, or whether there is a hidden meaning. For example, saying: "Oh, that's a really intelligent thing to say!" and meaning the opposite, will be lost on many people with NLD. The use of humor is a powerful tool in so many life situations. We use it to get across an otherwise negative message ("Hey, who died and left you Emperor of the world?!"), to lighten a serious situation ("There's no bread? Oh well, I guess we can always eat cake!"), to establish rapport, to increase intimacy, to cover up our insecurities, to gain an audience, to showcase our wit – the opportunities are endless. We tend to gravitate toward those who share a similar sense of humor, and sometimes have problems connecting with those who do not. It is not necessarily that individuals with NLD have no sense of humor; rather, they tend to laugh at physical comedy, or other direct and obvious situations, rather than something that requires the understanding of innuendos, double entendres, or the ability to visualize situations not previously directly experienced. It is also quite common for individuals with NLD to have poor understanding and use of timing, thus sharing an anecdote or, to them, humorous experience at an inopportune or inappropriate moment.

Use of analogy, metaphor

Most individuals with NLD are quite concrete in their language – they say what they mean, and they mean what they say, and they assume that everyone else does. So, when we say: "It's raining cats and dogs," they look for them. Metaphors such as the "learning cake" may well be lost on them, and they wonder why people are talking about flour and eggs when they want to know why they are having problems with their learning. Most good literature, poetry, plays, movies, etc. utilize metaphor and analogy, and in high school and beyond, most reading comprehension requires an understanding of nuance and inference. Individuals with NLD can often manage fine when reading factual texts for information-gathering purposes. However, the interpretation of an author's use of symbolic language (e.g. "the inner eye of solitude," "the slings and arrows of outrageous fortune," etc.) may completely elude them.

Turn-taking in conversation

Because of their good vocabulary and general knowledge, most individuals with NLD can "hold forth" and conduct monologues on a number of topics, without recognizing or acknowledging that true communicative language requires a response from the other party or parties. Having an idea of how long one can speak before letting another person have a turn is a nonverbal skill. Judging how long to speak before allowing someone else to have a say is a skill that most of us acquire without being aware of it. We are also usually okay with "reading" someone else's body language and facial expressions (e.g. leaning forward, opening the mouth, taking a breath…) as signs that they wish to say something. For individuals with NLD, we find ourselves needing to interrupt them in order to take our turn.

Body language

There are certain unwritten "rules" regarding how we act when we are speaking that assist others to interpret the meaning of what we are saying; for example, making and maintaining appropriate eye contact, physical distance from the speaker, touching someone as we speak, "tightness" of body (e.g. arms folded, jaw clenched, shoulders shrugged, etc.). We utilize similar cues when "reading" another's mood or intent, and when trying to predict what is coming next. We need not only to notice, but more importantly to interpret correctly, such body language as someone turning away, getting up and walking out, approaching with an embrace, acting in a sexually provocative way, looking positive/negative, changing mood, and so on. This permits us to predict and to choose what subsequent responses are most likely to be appropriate.

Facial expressions

Observation, recognition as significant, and interpretation of people's facial expressions are critical in social interactions. By doing so, we can often be quite successful in determining the speaker's feelings and therefore being able to predict what is likely to happen in the immediate future, allowing us to plan a response. Important in this regard are such things as: recognizing that someone is frowning, smiling, closing eyes, rolling eyes, pursing lips, raising an eyebrow, widening eyes, winking, clenching cheek muscles, and so on. These expressions are also helpful in figuring out whether an individual is projecting the same feeling as that expressed in the words he or she is speaking, and in his or her tone of voice.

Rhythm and rhyme

These are nonword aspects of language that are especially important in the early stages of reading acquisition, in order that a child can learn to recognize patterns of language that will help to predict what is coming next; they are also important memory aids.

Social interactions

Because of difficulties recognizing and interpreting visual cues, including facial expressions and gestures, and because of problems adjusting their verbal output (e.g. vocabulary, tone of voice, subject of conversation, turn-taking, etc.) to be appropriate for different circumstances, children with NLD frequently encounter difficulties in a variety of social situations. They do not notice that others are becoming impatient, losing interest, experiencing different emotions, needing personal space, wanting a turn, and countless other visual markers that cue a range of responsive behaviors.

It is often reported by parents and teachers that children with NLD have more success interacting with adults or younger children than they do with their peers. When adults recognize an inappropriate tone in an interaction, they tend to adjust their roles accordingly, and relate to an NLD child as they would to another adult. Or they may verbalize their observations, which cues the NLD youngster with certain expectations: "Tony, you're going on and on and no one is interested. Please talk about something else!" or "Katie, you're not looking at me when I'm talking to you." Younger children perceive an older child with NLD as simply someone older, and do not differentiate between what would be normal for, say, an 11-year-old as opposed to an adult. They therefore are more tolerant of being spoken to as if they are younger, regardless of who is doing the talking. Children with NLD may, however, have problems maintaining friendships with their age peers for many different reasons. For example: their interests are often quite different and/or are pursued at a far deeper level than normal; they are not interested in those things that fascinate their peers and are unwilling to feign interest; they tend to lecture and monologue, often using vocabulary that is adult-like and often sounds old-fashioned; and they frequently are unable to adjust their verbal interactions in terms of both content and delivery style for their specific and different "audiences." In short, they do not always know what they need to do to get people to like them.

Input/output issues

It is often observed that individuals with NLD not only do not recognize nonverbal aspects of communication in others, but that they do not utilize them themselves. In other words, their outward appearance may be devoid of a variety of cues that allow us to interpret their feelings, thoughts, and intentions. Thus, they frequently come across as flat, lacking affect, robotic, awkward, and very difficult to "read." This is most likely due to some difficulties with insight and introspection, along with problems picking up cues from within as to emotional and physical state. Also, for some individuals, it appears that they do not process well the proprioceptive feedback from various parts of the body (e.g. face, skin, feet, hands) that would normally tell us much about how we appear to other people. It is important to bear in mind that we need to acknowledge and work with both receptive and expressive facets of nonverbal communication.

Familial factors

Research has long indicated that learning disabilities tend to run in families, whether this is due to genetic heritability factors, social learning, habit, or a combination of these. Discussions with clinicians who work with individuals with NLD tend to confirm this to be the case. There is a good probability that one or both parents of a youngster with NLD will also themselves show some signs of NLD. Bearing in mind that we learn our communication skills primarily at home from very powerful models, it is necessary to explore and take account of the fact that problems with nonverbal aspects of communication, behavior, and social skills may be being modeled within the family.

Interactions between infants and their primary caregivers rely on sensory cues (e.g. visual images, smells, tactile input, sounds, auditory patterns, etc.), and are reinforced and "learned" by reciprocal reinforcement. "Reading" the patterns of a baby's vocalizations, facial expressions and body movements is something that does not come easily, even to those of us without pattern recognition problems. Attempting to interpret a preverbal youngster's signals and responding accordingly are even more difficult for someone with a nonverbal learning disability. Thus, any problems in utilizing or interpreting such cues may well affect attachment behaviors and subsequent relationships within the family from a very early stage. It is, therefore, often important for parents to work on their own nonverbal behaviors so that they can model them appropriately for their children.

During the course of having a child assessed, many parents and teachers recognize similar patterns in themselves, either currently or from past experience at school. This sometimes results in an ability to identify with the child's experiences. The positive side of this is the obvious empathy that it can engender, which helps us to understand what these children are going through and, it is hoped, to see what we can provide that we believe helped us, as well as how we can protect them from the more negative experiences we may have endured. However, there may be a negative aspect to over-identification, in that this can sometimes lead to over-protectiveness which contributes to a child's lack of trust in his or her own abilities and interferes dramatically with the development of self-sufficiency and independence.

Global difficulties

Individuals with NLD often experience difficulties with a number of global, abstract abilities that are both hard to operationalize and hard to measure.

- *Intuition*: the "gut" feeling or "sixth sense" we have about situations or people or problem-solving; knowing something without having to be told.

- *Initiative*: resourcefulness; starting something without being told to do it; taking the lead in an activity.

- *Insight*: that elusive "aha!" phenomenon that indicates that the light bulb just went on and we suddenly understand a pattern.

- *Imagination*: the ability to be able to think about something that has not actually happened; creative and often hypothetical thinking.

- *Integration*: the ability to see both the forest and the trees, and to be able to switch back and forth between both; the ability to be able to put parts together and create a whole, and to be able to apply a theoretical concept in a real-life situation.

- *Interpretation*: the ability to go beyond the facts in order to make inferences, draw conclusions, suggest meanings, and to make sense of something.

- *Independence*: the ability to function autonomously, without needing to be waited on, told what to do, prompted to do it, or supervised.

When professionals are assessing and diagnosing learning difficulties and intellectual exceptionalities, we need to rely on standardized test instruments with reliable and valid norms, so that we can legitimately determine where an individual functions relative to an age-related peer group, and so that we can compare results across different tests and different periods of time. All of the global difficulties listed here defy quantitative measurement. We simply do not have instruments to test them. However, we all know them when we experience or observe them, and we all know when they are lacking.

The assessment of NLD is incomplete without some attempt to assess these very important variables. Those of us who are experienced in formal assessment have developed a way of doing our job that alerts us when we need to adjust what we are used to doing in order to accommodate difficulties on the part of those with whom we are interacting. Those of us who are parents with more than one child are fully aware that we adjust our parenting to accommodate different personalities and temperaments among our children. Teachers recognize children who respond very differently from other students in day-to-day classroom activities. Both parents and teachers are often heard to say: "I know there's something, but I just can't put my finger on it…" Even though these experiences cannot be quantified, more subjective information can be helpful, and even essential, in order to paint the full picture of how individuals with NLD actually function, along with their strengths and weaknesses in everyday situations. Anecdotes, comparisons, opinions, casual observations, and even our own feelings, are all legitimate data when it comes to understanding and managing NLD, and should form part of every thorough assessment. Therefore it is important for professionals to explore these areas, and if they do not do so, for parents and teachers to document their observations and to try to ensure that the information is included in the overall picture.

Maturity and experiences will impact on all of the global issues outlined here. While we can, and should, teach and encourage independence, and perhaps to some degree can find ways to teach integration skills, the others remain elusive to external influences, and may simply be part of a broad range of characteristics that we have to live with, rather than be able to change in any significant way.

Chapter 3

ASSESSMENT AND DIAGNOSIS
OF NLD

General issues in diagnosis

The assessment and diagnosis of any type of learning disability or other condition can be important for many reasons: validation of a parent's and/or teacher's concerns; explanation of a group of symptoms and signs; provision of a statement regarding causal factors; acquisition of funding for special education; class placement; eligibility for disability allowances; access to program modifications and accommodation; provision of a direction for intervention; understanding of the longer-term implications; explanation as to why previous interventions may not have been successful, and so on.

The common starting points in the referral process for assessment of any kind of learning difficulty are those observable learning, behavioral or emotional difficulties identified by parents and teachers; for example: "Jenna is struggling with decoding words and understanding vocabulary;" "Tyler has great verbal abilities, but can't put his ideas down on paper," "He's fine in the language arts areas, but has never done well in math;" "She simply can't get her projects organized;" "Matthew is just not motivated." We then begin to search for the cognitive "patterns" or learning profiles that underlie these various manifestations, asking questions and gathering data with the dual purposes of exploring possible causal factors and proposing remedial approaches.

Unfortunately, many practitioners stop at the point where they simply confirm a discrepancy between an individual's cognitive potential (at least average in key areas of thinking and reasoning) and his or her academic achievement, without clearly linking specific psychological process deficits to the identified learning difficulties, and sometimes even without ruling out other possible reasons for an individual's failure to perform at expected levels (e.g. anxiety, situational stress, environmental factors, family conflict, inadequate teaching, physical illness, non-attendance at school, etc.). Parents and teachers alike are frequently left frustrated by the assessment experience, since it either does not tell them anything they did not already know, or substitutes their daily experiences with incomprehensible jargon that they are unable either to fathom or to translate into meaningful interventions. It is therefore important that a thorough evaluation is undertaken in order to explore the full breadth and depth of strengths, as well as weaknesses, so that relevant directions for remedial and compensatory strategies can follow.

The *identification* of a learning disability appears logically to be within the purview of educators, and may well be appropriate for a variety of professionals. Given a checklist of various signs and symptoms, it is also deceptively simple for any interested party to express an opinion regarding the presence of a wide range of disorders and disabilities. However, because of the neurological and neuropsychological roots of learning disabilities (LD), as well as the possibility of other factors causing a child's learning difficulties, it is important to understand that an accurate *diagnosis* goes far beyond simply identifying a cluster of associated signs or symptoms and labeling them, otherwise known as the *formulation* of that diagnosis. It also includes the communication of that information to an individual and/or his or her agents by someone who has the appropriate credentials and training to take responsibility for a thorough assessment, the knowledge base to understand and infer causality, and the skills and experience for prescribing appropriate interventions. In many North American jurisdictions, the act of communicating a diagnosis is considered to be a "controlled act" and is restricted under legislation to specific professions (e.g. medicine, psychology) because it has potential for harm. Consider the implications of an error in diagnosis that could lead to inappropriate intervention or to no intervention at all. Thus, both the formulation and communication of a diagnosis need to be taken extremely seriously, and exercised only with utmost caution.

As with other childhood conditions, there are frequently many professionals, as well as parents, who are familiar with a range of problem areas and who are well able to provide an opinion or a judgement as to what might be the cause of a child's difficulties. In fact, it is essential to collect information from as many people as possible in the formulation phase of diagnosis. In these days of the Internet, in particular, many of us are very well read and informed, particularly if there is clearly something affecting our children that we feel some responsibility to fix. Because of different biases in knowledge and training, however, the probability of a particular opinion being given, even with the same symptom presentation, will vary depending on the background of the particular professional involved. For example, while a psychological service provider may interpret a given set of symptoms as nonverbal learning disability (NLD), a psychiatrist or neurologist may see the same set as Asperger's Syndrome, an occupational therapist as a Developmental Coordination Disorder or a Sensory Integration Disorder, and a speech-language pathologist as a Semantic-Pragmatic Language Disorder. It is not uncommon for parents of children with NLD to receive more than one, apparently conflicting, diagnosis, although it is always quite possible that more than one condition co-exist in what has been described as "the syndrome mix" (Kutscher 2005).

Another facet of diagnosis, albeit a slightly ugly one, is political. Those of us who have worked within the education system, especially at times when resources are scarce, know only too well of situations where certain diagnoses are acceptable and encouraged, while others are minimized or ignored. These situations universally involve funding for special education programs and/or staff. For example, if a ministry, department, board or district of education decides that it will provide financial support for children with Asperger's Syndrome, autism, and Attention Deficit Hyperactive Disorder, but not for NLD, then there will be few NLD diagnoses in that jurisdiction and an increase in the number of students "diagnosed" with those other disorders. This does not necessarily mean that the diagnoses are fraudulent, but simply that those test results supporting the "acceptable" diagnoses tend to be highlighted and used to justify a particular label that will guarantee a needy child appropriate resources for his or her education. This type of manipulation of test results will cease only when there is a different and more equitable funding base for all children with special needs, rather than essentially pitting one family against another.

DSM-IV diagnoses

There are many, perhaps even the vast majority of, practitioners in the field of psychology and medicine who rely on diagnoses prescribed by the American Psychiatric Association's *Diagnostic and Statistical Manual of Mental Disorders* (American Psychiatric Association 1994), currently in its fourth edition (DSM-IV):

- Reading Disorder
- Mathematics Disorder
- Disorder of Written Expression
- Learning Disorder Not Otherwise Specified (NOS).

All of these are defined as skill levels ("reading achievement," "mathematical ability," and "writing skills") that are "substantially below those expected given the person's chronological age, measured intelligence, and age-appropriate education." Additional criteria are that the disturbances in learning should significantly interfere with "academic achievement or activities of daily living" (p.46) that involve these abilities, and that they be in excess of difficulties that would normally be associated with sensory deficits (e.g. in vision or hearing).

Given the extent to which DSM-IV is utilized, and sometimes idealized, within the mental health professions, it is hardly surprising that so many practitioners believe that an adequate assessment of LD consists of a measure of academic achievement, a measure of "intelligence," and little more, with diagnosis based simply upon a discrepancy between the two.

Quite apart from the problem that many of us have conceptualizing a learning problem as a "mental disorder," the labels provided by this nomenclature are restrictive and simplistic. For example, "mathematics disorder" does not begin to address the vastness and complexity of possibilities when it comes to pinpointing the pattern of strengths and weaknesses that could be contributing to a poor grade on a report card. A child with primary language problems usually has trouble with the translation of mathematical concepts and operations into the "language" of math, and may not understand that "minus," "subtract," "take away," "give to," "reduce by," "less than," and so on, all represent the same change in quantity. Difficulties with visualization will lead to trouble manipulating quantity inside one's head, as in: "There are six sheep in the pen; two sheep leave, and four more enter. How many sheep are then in the pen?" or "Jack is taller than Joe, and shorter than John. Who is the smallest?" In addition, memory problems in any modality can affect all branches of math (e.g. algebra, geometry, trigonometry, calculus, data management, measurement, and so on), not simply the four basic arithmetic operations.

A diagnosis of any kind generally implies cause, as in: "I believe that this problem is caused by..." which in turn leads to suggestions for intervention. Unfortunately, the DSM-IV LD diagnoses merely reiterate what is already known, usually from information provided by the individual and/or parents, teachers and other professionals. Simply adding the label does not enlighten, nor does it provide direction for remediation.

It is also of great concern that there is often refusal on the part of many professionals (including psychological service providers, educators, some medical practitioners, etc.) specifically to recognize or diagnose a NLD because it is not stated specifically as such in DSM-IV. There have been many parents who have been told that there is no such diagnosis, and that NLD therefore does not exist. Based on several decades of consistent research, there is a common understanding within the disciplines of psychology, neurology, occupational therapy, speech-language pathology, and education as to what constitutes a learning disability. Many nonverbal psychological processes are clearly defined, quantifiable, and valid. Given an appropriate assessment that produces relevant data, there should therefore be no reason why a diagnosis of NLD cannot be reliably formulated and communicated.

Diagnostic indicators of NLD

The first concrete diagnostic indicator that NLD may well be a possibility is found in the child's cognitive profile, as measured by one of the standardized tests, such as the Wechsler Scales, the Woodcock-Johnson Tests of Cognitive Ability, the Stanford-Binet, the Kaufman Assessment Battery for Children, or other such battery. The most typical pattern on the Wechsler scales, for example, shows a significant discrepancy between the Verbal Comprehension and Perceptual Reasoning scales, in favor of the former. In other words, the NLD child may show relatively few, if any, deficits on verbal comprehension subtests, and perhaps would be seen as strong, very strong, or sometimes even gifted in areas such as general knowledge, verbal concept formation, vocabulary, and social problem-solving. The latter – for example, the Wechsler Intelligence Scale for Children Third (WISC-III) or Fourth Edition (WISC-IV) Comprehension subtest – may well be particularly important in the differential diagnosis of Asperger's Syndrome and this will be discussed below. If using the WISC-IV, there is often some merit in adding a couple of subtests from the WISC-III, specifically Object Assembly and Picture Arrangement, to allow examiners to observe the individual with NLD involved in more hands-on problem-solving, and to see first-hand the processing struggles that are evident, even when the final product is correct.

As explained in more detail under the different subtypes later in the guide, while a verbal comprehension–perceptual reasoning discrepancy on the WISC-IV is usually a starting point for suspecting NLD, it is important to examine the detailed psychoeducational profile before proceeding with further differential diagnosis. There are, in fact, a number of children with NLD who do *not* show a significant discrepancy between their verbal comprehension and perceptual reasoning scales, sometimes due to an unexpectedly high or low subtest score or two. For example, some children score extremely low in social problem-solving, which may reduce the overall verbal composite score, at the same time using their verbal strengths to help them work through one or more of the untimed "nonverbal" tasks, perhaps resulting in a strong score on, for example, the subtest requiring understanding picture concepts. Yet others may produce extremely low scores on the subtests measuring speed while showing average results on measures of verbal comprehension and perceptual reasoning. When using the WISC-III, it is often more useful to compare Index scores for Verbal Comprehension and Perceptual Organization, or Verbal Comprehension and Processing Speed, rather than to examine only the Verbal–Performance discrepancy. The Kaufman ABC-II provides the chance to examine the difference between a child's ability to process sequential versus simultaneous information, with the resulting opportunity to differentiate different types of pattern recognition problems. Children with NLD may be expected to do better on the tests of sequential reasoning than they do on the simultaneous scale which requires more integration and visual-spatial reasoning.

Criteria for diagnosis of NLD

Under the definition of LD outlined earlier, the following criteria would therefore need to be met for a diagnosis of a NLD.

Thinking and reasoning skills at least average

This means that there should be documented evidence that the individual has at least one major area of thinking and reasoning that reaches the criterion for "average." For most widely used tests with a mean of 100 and a standard deviation of 15, this is usually taken to mean a score of 80 or above, although many practitioners prefer to use the cut-off of one standard deviation, which is a score of 85 or above. It is important to note that there are many different and valid measures of "thinking and reasoning" skills, and that clinicians need to be prepared to back up their opinions with more than one test result. However, contrary to popular lay belief, it is not necessary for an individual's *overall* intelligence quotient (IQ) score to fall in the commonly accepted "average" or above ranges for the diagnosis of a LD to be made. In other words, an overall IQ score that is below the 80–85 range could still mean that an individual may have some major measures of thinking and reasoning that fall within the average band. For most NLD children, the strength(s) in thinking and reasoning are most likely to be found in the verbal areas – in measures of abstract and/or applied reasoning abilities. The Woodcock-Johnson III Tests of Cognitive Ability have a subscale called "Thinking Ability" that takes into account both verbal and nonverbal reasoning, which can be compared with either Verbal Ability or Cognitive Efficiency, the latter of which is frequently weak in NLD children. However, it may be the case that those children whose difficulties are primarily in visual-motor areas have relatively stronger scores on measures of visual pattern recognition or nonverbal concept formation that may fall in the broad average range, and even perhaps result in a lack of significant discrepancy between verbal and nonverbal scales.

Multiple "intelligences"

Identification of NLD may well be better pinpointed were it possible to assess in any reliable, valid, and standardized way a range of "intelligences" and reasoning skills beyond the widely used tests of verbal, quantitative, and visual-spatial abilities. For example, Gardner's (1999) theory of multiple intelligences allows for the consideration of such additional concepts as:

- kinesthetic intelligence: using mental abilities to coordinate bodily movements

- musical intelligence: performance, composition, and appreciation of musical patterns

- interpersonal intelligence: the capacity to understand the emotions, intentions, and desires of other people that allows us to interact with others

- intrapersonal intelligence: the ability to appreciate one's own feelings, fears, and motivations

- naturalist intelligence: recognize, categorize, and draw upon certain features of the environment.

It is tantalizing to consider exploring a person's individual mosaic of abilities from such a multifaceted perspective, and certainly holds great promise for understanding not only the weaknesses but also the strengths of people with NLD. However, quantification of the wide range of "normal" (and hence acceptable) attributes would definitely be a contentious issue.

Impairments in psychological processes related to learning

This means that there should be documented evidence that the individual has measurable impairment in at least one major area of nonverbal processing, including, but not limited to, visual/motor/tactile memory and attention; visual-motor and/or fine motor processing speed; pragmatic language difficulties; perceptual-motor processing; visual-spatial processing; executive functions (e.g. planning, monitoring, selective focusing, and other organizational abilities). These processing impairments should be logically connected to the individual's actual, observable learning deficits, in terms of being *causal* in nature. The range of potential assessment instruments to measure nonverbal psychological processes is, of course, quite broad, although it is hard to find measures that are free from the ubiquitous verbal mediation that assists most of us to solve problems. However, in general, a thorough assessment would include measures of visual-spatial processes (attention, short-term memory, long-term memory, accuracy/speed, discrimination, sequencing, etc.), fine motor ability (speed, dexterity, handedness, left–right discrimination, etc.), visual-motor integration (copying of linguistic and nonlinguistic stimuli, eye–hand coordination, etc.), executive functioning (planning ability, etc.), in addition to basic language testing that could tease out pragmatics from other, more obvious verbal abilities, such as vocabulary and general knowledge. Many of these psychological processes are, of course, measured in the course of a basic cognitive assessment. While even one or two low scores (sometimes a single subtest, sometimes clusters of subtest scores) are indicative of significant weakness in specific areas of functioning, it is necessary to provide further back-up with additional assessment data, observation, and/or reports from other professionals. In addition, it is necessary to look for specific patterns of abilities that are related to and therefore can logically predict the individual's pattern of learning problems. A new test battery, the Wechsler Non-verbal Scale, contains a variety of nonverbal tests, including visual pattern completion, visual-motor sequencing, visual-motor integration, puzzle completion, and logical visual sequencing, most or all of which would be predictably weak in children with NLD. However, without the opportunity to compare the results of these tests with some language-based assessment, there could be some confusion between NLD and some more generalized developmental delay.

It's not what you do…

Some children's test performance is affected more by *how* they perform the test, not *what* they say or do, resulting in scores that are not particularly different from the norm for their age, but reflecting a somewhat circuitous and less efficient route to get there. Others are more ponderous, and slower to perform any test that is timed, and it is important to differentiate those children who are successful on all items but who do not gain bonus time points from those who perform some items very quickly but make errors on others. This appears to be especially necessary for children from about age 13 and up, since some test results are affected quite significantly by such time bonuses, or lack thereof, with the score often reflecting a child's processing *speed* rather than actual competence at a given task. It is always important to consider this issue when interpreting test scores.

For clinicians, it is vitally important to take a broader look at the child's *overall* presenting profile, including anecdotal information from parents and teachers, and to observe the individual's behavior extremely carefully during the course of the assessment in order to pick up important processing difficulties that may not be reflected in the actual scores themselves.

It is sometimes the case for individuals with NLD that they score relatively well when tested on *individual* academic subskills. For example, when they are tested on spelling, or multiplication, or definitions, they may appear to be quite average or even better. Even when they are found to be deficient in a specific area, they can sometimes be remediated in that specific area with some apparent degree of success. However, they do not appear to generalize or to be able to use these skills in more complex task areas. This emphasizes the fact that it is the *integration* of the skills that reflects the deficits, and not the specific level of ability *per se*. The integration aspects are sometimes difficult to measure objectively, and often must be inferred.

Because of these more subjective issues, it is important to emphasize that a much broader range of observational and anecdotal information needs to be gathered, rather than limiting assessment to formal testing alone.

Information processing profile model

Some of us may believe that an underlying LD *causes* problems with the acquisition of visual-motor skills, fine motor control, primary language abilities, and so on, and hence difficulties in any learning situation. Others may argue that problems with visual-motor skills, or fine motor control, or primary language abilities are what actually *constitute* the LD. Either way, anomalies or abnormalities in the underlying neurological "map" will certainly disrupt the normal acquisition and development of any or all secondary areas of learning, such as reading, math, and written expression. This underlying profile of psychological processes, which is quite likely to be different for each individual, leads to a pattern of secondary learning deficits that we see in the classroom and other learning environments, including the family, social context, workplace, and life in general. Hence, once we understand an individual's information processing profile with its unique strengths and weaknesses, we can start to predict the kinds of learning situations that will most likely cause problems. Only then can we truly begin to understand the types of interventions that will be required in order to remediate and/or compensate appropriately.

If we *begin* by exploring the underlying neuropsychological or psychoeducational profiles of individuals exhibiting learning difficulties in order to look for patterns of strength and weakness, it is possible to *predict* from those profiles what types of learning situations are likely to prove challenging for each particular, and perhaps even unique, pattern of learning differences.

This means that, while we pay attention to and are guided in our assessment process by the initial descriptions of the individual's presenting problems, we need to put them on the side-burner while we explore and identify each individual's underlying pattern of abilities, along with various other components (such as personality factors, family and school contexts, emotional make-up, etc.). We can then see whether understanding the resulting specific pattern, or profile, helps us to predict the pattern of learning problems that individual is currently having or is likely to have in the future. Using this process, we not only validate the reasons for initial referral, but also have a basis upon which to initiate interventions, whether remedial or compensatory, that are likely to effect some changes in the presenting problems, and it is hoped, to prevent future problems from developing.

As an example, an individual whose short-term visual memory is weak, but whose auditory memory is strong, would be predicted to do well in learning situations where the information is presented orally and where learning is measured by regurgitation of this information by oral means (e.g. rote memory of multiplication tables, retrieval of facts, oral expressive vocabulary, and so on). However, this same individual would be expected to do more poorly when asked to process information presented visually (e.g. on a chalkboard, slides, written text material, etc.), and subsequently to reproduce this same information in a visually based format (e.g. in writing, keyboarding, model reproduction, etc.) or even simply trying to recall what has been seen in order to compare it with a number of different options (e.g. multiple-choice tests, matching tasks, etc.). Such a pattern would be expected to cause difficulties in subject areas such as written work of any kind, especially in a second language, where there would be less familiarity, especially with the use of visual markers such as accents, umlauts, and cedillas. Written language based on visual symbols that have no phonetic associations (such as Chinese and Japanese) would also be predicted to be a problem area. Subjects that include mapping, graphs, diagrams, and other overtly visual information, whether factual or symbolic, prove to be mystifying territory for individuals with visual processing difficulties.

Visualization

A common information processing difficulty in individuals with NLD involves the process of visualization. There are three different aspects of this process, essentially related to past, present and future contexts.

1. *Past*: We may be required to revisualize something for which we already have an existing visual image – i.e. something that we have seen or experienced before. This would involve such circumstances as remembering the spelling of a phonetically irregular word, recalling routes we have previously driven, picturing someone's face, recreating the memory of an event, and myriad similar situations. Thus, individuals with NLD frequently have difficulties with tasks requiring recall from visual memory, affecting such areas as written work, written math processes, directions, and so on. However, they are less likely to have problems with visualization if there is a pre-existing visual image to be recalled, than if there is a requirement for a visual image to be created.

2. *Present*: We are sometimes called upon to visualize something in real time – for example, we might be asked to picture three elephants and to add another two elephants, to think about what we have to pack in our backpacks, to match a face to a name, or to "look over" our work to see if it matches the way it is supposed to look. Problems with such immediate visualization will hamper information processing, especially in the absence of accompanying verbal explanations and/or instructions.

3. *Future*: There are many occasions when we need to visualize something that has not yet happened. This ability helps us to imagine, to create options, to foresee consequences, to predict others reactions, to plan for contingencies, to dream, or to engage in a range of hypothetical thoughts. Individuals who have difficulties picturing situations that have not yet been experienced will therefore be expected to have problems with planning and organizing, with predicting the behavior of others, with anticipating outcomes, with "between-the-lines" issues, and other circumstances requiring the mental construction of never-before experienced situations or events. Children are often expected to learn hypothetically, by imagining what it would be like, for example, to touch a hot stove, rather than actually to experience what could be a negative or even dangerous consequence. This has many implications for parenting, since we often try to parent verbally, without intending to follow through with action, especially when that action might be considered to be negative for the child. In addition, most therapeutic approaches require a certain degree of visualization – whether it be for teaching relaxation techniques, anticipating change, picturing different outcomes, etc., and difficulties in this area can significantly affect success.

Assessment issues in young children

Psychological assessment instruments are sometimes somewhat limiting when attempting to assess for NLD in preschool and kindergarten-aged children, since there is a broad range of what is considered to be developmentally normal for children under the age of seven. Such instruments as the Wechsler Primary and Preschool Scale of Intelligence Third Edition (WPPSI-III), the Stanford-Binet V, the Kaufman Assessment Battery for Children Second Edition, etc., can certainly provide extremely useful information with respect to current functioning levels, and can point to areas for potential intervention. They may not, however, be as useful in predicting the pervasive nature of some areas of weakness. The new Wechsler Non-verbal Scale is appropriate for use with individuals as young as four years of age, although when using this instrument, measures of language function would also be necessary in order to differentiate between NLD and overall developmental delays.

Children, however young, who show significant deficits in one or more specific areas, however, need to be flagged as "at risk," with the appropriate professionals (e.g. occupational therapists for fine motor and visual-motor problems, speech-language pathologists for language processing difficulties, audiologists for central auditory processing issues, etc.) providing service as early as possible. It is sometimes the case that children who are retested at a later date may well show quite a different intellectual profile, especially when they have received some timely therapy.

Documentation of a LD

Both parents and teachers alike are frequently concerned about the information contained (or not contained) in psychological and psychoeducational reports. It goes without saying that a very thorough assessment, along with appropriate documentation, is required in support of a diagnosis of any type of LD. Any diagnostic report should include all of the following components, unless a valid rationale is provided for not doing so:

- information about home language use (original language, dialect, language(s) spoken in the home, etc.)

- relevant medical/developmental/family history, including results of any vision/hearing evaluations

- educational history, including information about remedial programs, special class placements, or other support that have been provided

- relevant information from other professional evaluations (e.g. speech-language, occupational therapy, educational consultant, etc.), including previous psychological assessments

- a statement regarding the validity of the assessment

- behavioral observations during the testing session, as well as available observations (both anecdotal and from rating scales) from parents, teachers, classroom visits, etc.

- reporting and interpretation of formal test results, including a description of the individual's strengths and needs, an indication of how the observed pattern of abilities and achievement demonstrates the presence of a specific disability, and adequately documented evidence as to the cause of the learning difficulties

- a specific, clear, diagnostic statement that the individual has a LD

- based on the individual's strengths and needs, recommendations, suggestions and indications for further action and intervention in the areas of skill instruction, compensatory strategies, and self-advocacy skills, along with requirements for appropriate accommodations at home, and in school, community and/or workplace settings

- signature of an appropriately qualified professional who should be present (preferably in person, or in real-time audio or visual connection) when oral diagnostic reports are delivered.

Appropriately documented, informed consent for psychological assessment should always be obtained in advance from the individual concerned, or from his or her parents or legal guardians, by the individual who will be conducting the assessment. In addition to information regarding the assessment procedures themselves, such informed consent should include an explanation regarding: the potential release of information and/or the report to any third party; the potential distribution and storage of the assessment information and documentation, including circulation within a school system or inclusion in the student's legal record; the individual's rights regarding withholding or withdrawal of consent; and the right of direct access to the qualified individual who is responsible for the diagnosis.

Many assessment reports contain profession-specific jargon or mumbo-jumbo that means nothing to those individuals who must use these documents to support everything from special education placements to parenting interventions to disability insurance claims. "So what?" is probably the most frequently asked question, after "What does this word mean?"

It is critical for the author to communicate information in a way that it can be understood by the intended "audience." We are way beyond the time when psychologists and others wrote reports only for physicians, or other psychological service providers, or even their graduate supervisors. Parents are almost always the child's primary case managers, and as such need to be able to understand clearly what the results of a report mean. This means that it is insufficient to say, for example, "His perceptual organizational skills are below average." It is vital that everyone understands what this statement *implies* or *predicts* or *connects with* in terms of an individual's daily life at school, at home, or elsewhere, and how it can be translated into concrete and realistic recommendations for action.

It is necessary for parents to be confident enough to approach the author of the report for an explanation of anything that is not understood, for clarification of terms, and for questions regarding the implications of any statements contained therein.

It is also critical for professionals to remember that the individual frequently reads his or her own report – maybe not immediately if he or she is a child, but potentially in several years' time. It is a reasonable rule-of-thumb for professionals never to write anything that they would not be comfortable with a client reading. Practitioners should never forget that an assessment is an intervention, and as such can have far-reaching consequences.

In addition, there are clearly teachers, psychologists, physicians, and other professionals who exhibit a pattern of attributes consistent with NLD, and who rely heavily on their verbal skills to manage their day-to-day functioning and issues. It is important to bear this in mind when attempting to explain NLD, helping parents understand what the implications are, and suggesting strategies that might help. The use of analogies, body language, subtle nonverbal indications of expectations, or other nonverbal cues, needs to be monitored, and it will be necessary to check out regularly that good communication has, in fact, taken place, in order to prevent misunderstandings and misinterpretations. Ensuring that verbal communication is direct, clear, and free from ambiguities will be most helpful. Like their children, however, there may be a strong tendency for parents with NLD to understand, remember, and repeat the verbal information given to them by professionals – and yet not notice when it is appropriate to utilize and actually implement this information in order to effect change. It is important for those of us who are professionals to practice what we preach, and to translate our verbal feedback clearly into actual *action*, at the very least by giving demonstrations or concrete examples, rather than sticking with high-level and official-sounding jargon.

It is important to be aware that a specific diagnosis is not a prerequisite to providing assistance for a child with academic or behavioral issues. Even if a child's difficulties do not meet specific diagnostic requirements, an understanding of the pattern of strengths and weaknesses can help determine appropriate remedial and compensatory strategies, even for children whose impairments are relatively mild.

Chapter 4

PATTERN RECOGNITION AND NLD

Most research on nonverbal learning disabilities (NLD), in particular that conducted by neuropsychologists, is focused on trying to discover the causal factors, especially in terms of which parts and pathways of the brain are involved, and looking for various anatomical, physiological, neurological, biochemical, genetic, and/or environmental factors that correlate with different manifestations of learning difficulties. For most of us, even those who have some training in basic brain-behavior patterns, the various theories, findings, and even language of the resulting articles are beyond understanding. The same can often be said for the reports that are generated for individuals with NLD, their parents and teachers, subsequent to a psychological assessment. It is very frustrating for even the best-motivated of us to try to translate this wealth of theories, assumptions, data, and conclusions into anything that is meaningful in our daily lives and in our grass-roots interactions with NLD children. "So what?" and "What does this actually mean in real life?" are questions frequently asked by those at the receiving end of feedbacks and assessment reports.

Brain-behavior research in the area of learning disability (LD) is clearly necessary and beneficial if we are ever truly to understand the complex functioning of the human mind, and there may well be some procedure, machine, or pill in the future that will revolutionize special education and render all other interventions obsolete. In the meantime, it is important to see if we can find a model of functioning that can help us not only to understand the mechanisms that underlie learning and contribute to various difficulties, but also that can provide a framework for useful assessments that lead us in directions for fruitful intervention.

General concept of pattern recognition

The model proposed here involves the basic concept of *pattern recognition* in the hope that it can provide an understandable basis from which to understand and predict the kinds of problems that underlie difficulties in processing and learning nonverbal information. It was Marshall McLuhan, the Canadian media analyst and philosopher, who said that in the midst of chaos, we seek patterns. A common-sense analysis of learning will quickly tell us that all learning is, in fact, pattern recognition, memory, and reproduction. Once we can reproduce a pattern from memory, whatever that pattern may be, we can be said to have "learned" it. In fact, patterns that are practiced and rehearsed over and over again eventually become automatic, and are believed to be stored as a "whole" unit within the central nervous system. From our own experiences, we know all about this phenomenon. Those of us fortunate enough to be fluent typists know that it is difficult to type out the alphabet, simply because that involves finger movements in a pattern that we are not used to using. Most of us can relate to the experience of going into "automatic pilot" when driving, ending up on a familiar route when we had intended to go somewhere different. Brushing our teeth, chanting a prayer, running, driving the car, breathing – all kinds of complex activities are programmed in our brains as one unit, and require little or no analysis of each of the small behaviors that make up the complex chain. In fact, if we are asked to think about one aspect only (for example, to breathe deeply during a doctor's examination), we may be temporarily thrown off, and the normally automatic task suddenly appears awkward or even difficult. Automatic pattern recognition and reproduction allow us to multitask. Our minds are elsewhere. We can walk and chew gum at the same time.

Even simpler organisms are programmed to recognize patterns that have crucial meaning for survival. Almost a half century ago, an article entitled "What the frog's eye tells the frog's brain" (Lettvin *et al.* 1959) pointed out that a frog is uniquely programmed to respond to a certain movement across its visual field, however complex the visual background may be, by swiftly extending its tongue. This basic act of pattern recognition followed by a purposeful behavior enables the frog to catch bugs, eat, and survive.

Our complex world requires us to recognize patterns in a wide range of different situations, each of which has its own unique properties and uses, and out of which we gradually make sense of the world in which we function. Human young require the longest time of any living species to acquire the information required to leave the "nest" and function autonomously away from parents, by learning to keep themselves safe and to acquire the necessities for survival which, in these technological times, seems to include knowing how to work a cell phone, a pager, and various other wireless devices, in addition to accessing shelter, water, nourishment, and other basics of life. If an individual is unable to recognize those patterns necessary for learning the skills required for survival, the world presents myriad dangers and the individual is unlikely to manage independently.

Quite apart from recognizing, as does the frog, those visual patterns that allow us to eat, we humans have to identify and utilize everything from those specific auditory patterns necessary to learn language, to the most complex social patterns required for interpersonal interaction needed in a variety of contexts, from the family to the classroom to the workplace to the world at large. The human brain is an amazing organ, capable of the most complex pattern analysis. While it can tolerate and adapt to a wide range and variety of inputs, there are many difficulties with this process of recognition, identification, analysis, reproduction, and memory of patterns that are quite likely to lead to problems in learning and behavior of all kinds.

If we can understand what patterns the brain is trying to recognize, learn, and remember, we can begin to predict what the consequences may be of disruptions in these various processes, and hence be able to plan for ways in which either to remediate or compensate for the difficulties or deficits that may result. So the focus here will be specifically on the relationship between pattern recognition and NLD in order to see whether this concept can help us understand better the kinds of learning problems these individuals exhibit and, more importantly, how to help.

For simplicity, pattern recognition as it relates to NLD is described below by modality. For each one, we examine the kinds of patterns that are important to recognize and remember, and what the implications are for learning if and when there are disruptions in that particular processing. In addition, the specific relevance of each aspect of pattern recognition for academic learning will be noted, although not exhaustively explored.

Auditory patterns

The auditory system, as are all sensory systems, is set up as a pattern recognition device. Each ear analyzes a sequence of discrete sounds that are translated from differences in air pressure on the ear drum to a system of mechanics and hydraulics to the electrical signals that fire up the acoustic nerve. At higher cognitive levels, the brain then combines the signals from both ears and interprets the resulting pattern. The complexity of this operation is mind-boggling. Those who would like more information on this topic are referred to such academic texts as Bregman 1994, and any up-to-date introductory psychology or audiology text book. For current purposes, we shall concentrate on a few elements of global auditory pattern recognition, even though this is recognized as being a little simplistic.

Recognition/reproduction of sounds for the acquisition of speech and language

Newborns have long been known to be able to process and distinguish linguistically meaningful sounds soon after birth (Moffitt 1971). While they are born able to reproduce the sounds of any potential language, as children develop, they filter out those sounds that are not meaningful as they begin to recognize and imitate their own mother tongue. Within the first few years of life, young children can recognize, remember, and reproduce sound patterns well enough to be able to understand and use most of the complexities of language. Those children who fail to develop this ability are clearly at a disadvantage when it comes to developing adequate verbal abilities to handle both academic and social learning tasks.

Early attachment behavior

The ability of young infants to recognize and prefer their primary caretaker's voice over others is clearly important for early attachment. Obviously, young babies are not attending as much to the content of the sound patterns as they are to such things as tone, amplitude, urgency, and so on – in other words, most of the nonverbal aspects of communication discussed previously. Appropriate attachment leads to the development of trust relationships, and a predictability in terms of having basic needs met, and hence is important for survival. Children who cannot distinguish the sound patterns associated with situations in which they can trust those around them are possibly at risk for later social vulnerability. In turn, as adults and parents, it is necessary to interpret the preverbal auditory signals of infants in order to attempt to meet their needs. For most of us, this is at best intelligent guesswork that still sometimes fails to comfort the child. For individuals who do not process auditory patterns well, or even at all, it can become a nightmare of stress, and perhaps interfere with the bonding and attachment processes.

Nonverbal communication

Quite apart from the need to decipher incoming speech sounds in order to understand basic patterns that make sense as words, there are many other sound patterns that are important in transmitting information. For example, even when we cannot actually hear the exact words someone is saying, or when another person is speaking a foreign language that has no familiarity to us, we are usually able to understand such things as the person's mood, level of arousal, urgency, and often even his or her intent, simply by noting such nonverbal cues as amplitude, intensity, and cadence (rise and fall). In fact, when we have to rely simply on the words without any other cues (such as, for example, in a plain email with no capitals, italics or "smilies," or in a message passed on by a third party, or when we do not pick up auditory pattern cues), there may well be misinterpretation and misunderstanding of the originator's message. Individuals with NLD often neither understand nor utilize nonverbal auditory patterns, and may use inappropriate levels of loudness, and/or sound quite monotonic or even sometimes robotic in their expressive speech.

Threat or danger

Again, apart from the linguistic content of a signal, there are many cues to be processed from sound patterns that will alert us to a potential threat or danger. The sound of someone's footsteps approaching, a siren, a smoke detector, a creaking door, an unusual sound in the house at night, a deep-throated growl from a dog, a sound that awakens us from sleep, a baby crying – all of these, and many more, are devoid of verbal content, but require recognition and interpretation. If we are unable to do so, our safety and security are at risk. Many children with NLD will often know at an intellectual level, and can even tell us, that a growling dog is dangerous and should be left alone, or that when the smoke detector or fire alarm go off, there are certain actions to perform. We are then surprised or shocked that the child keeps on playing with the growling dog, or does not react at the sound of the alarm. We need to understand that they are not actually processing the sound pattern, but will most likely respond only when they hear the *words* that we have trained them to recognize ("Hey, the dog's growling – leave him alone!" or "That's the fire alarm! Quick, out of the house!").

Implications for academic learning

Obviously, listening skills and the ability to recognize patterns in what we hear are both critical for all classroom activities, since the majority of teaching is verbally based. If there is any difficulty with or interruption in the auditory signal, as seen for example in children with central auditory processing problems, there is an increased chance of difficulty in all areas of learning. Language arts subjects are particularly at risk in view of the need to integrate auditory input with reading and writing skills. How a word sounds is an important cue to how it looks. Difficulties in recognition of rhythm patterns may affect such subjects as music, dance, physical education and drama, as well as some aspects of auditory memory that could in turn affect the rote learning aspect of many different core subject areas, such as mathematics.

Language patterns

Individuals with NLD appear to have few, if any, difficulties processing basic language patterns that make up our grammar and syntax. For the most part, they do not mis-sequence words in sentences, and are generally very articulate, some-times extremely so, when it comes to expressing their thoughts in oral form. However, there is more to language patterns than the ability to understand sequences of words.

Pragmatics

The kinds of language patterns that cause more difficulty are those that are reflected more in terms of interactive discourse, and that require an understanding of such issues as the purpose of the conversation, turn-taking, active listening, predicting what another person needs to hear or is likely to say, and so on. We pick up these pragmatic, social language patterns in many ways, some of which are very subtle. We learn, with time and experiences, what to say to certain people at certain times, when to say it, and how to say it so that we can communicate our own needs and understand the needs of others. Life is a continuous learning process in this domain, and pretty much every conversation we have is new and different, requir-ing us to draw on all of our previous knowledge, and we need to be prepared to be flexible and innovative. We notice that someone has asked us a question, requiring an answer, even if the question does not start with why-what-where-who-how-when, as in "You coming?" or "Had enough?", simply by a change in sound pattern. We know the difference between a calm discussion and a heated argument. We know that a single word can express a whole thought ("Great!" "Oh!") and know enough to ask for more information, or stay quiet, depending on mood, context, etc. Individuals with NLD are often unaware of these language patterns, making conversation difficult.

Monologue or dialogue?

Most importantly, we learn the difference between monologue and dialogue. We recognize that interactive communication requires us to pause and to listen, as well as to speak, and we incorporate these activities into our daily conversational speech almost without thinking. We may notice that, as we are speaking, the other person is taking a breath and preparing to speak, which makes us cut short what we are saying. We watch for someone yawning, turning away, or speaking with finality, and know that we should be drawing the conversation to a close. These basic discourse patterns are often difficult for those with NLD to recognize, understand, acquire, and implement. They often lack that intuitive sense of needing to adapt what they want to say in order to fit in with the general "flow" of conversation, especially when more than one other person is involved, and sometimes fail to modulate loudness or tone to adapt to the specific interactional context. In fact, it is often necessary to interrupt the monologue in order to have any kind of two-way conversation.

When we do not, or cannot, notice, understand, predict, interpret, and/or use the wealth of information provided in language patterns, we are clearly at great disadvantage in all kinds of social situations.

Implications for academic learning

While it is obvious that language patterns are important for literary discourse, and hence written expression, the ability to debate issues and to be able to express one's point of view articulately are clearly important in all language-based subjects.

Visual/spatial patterns

The analysis of visual patterns is in most respects quite different from the analysis of the linear nature of auditory processing. We encode such variables as shape, color, distance, texture, movement, and so on, not only immediately, but also simultaneously. We are frequently able to revisit the same stimuli for a "second look." Our visual closure abilities enable us to visualize a "whole" object, even when we can only see some of the parts. Our visual memory allows us to recall "pictures" or patterns we have previously seen, and a wonderful, mysterious part of our mind enables us to create visual patterns that we have never, ever seen before. Try thinking about a purple elephant wearing a blue top hat, or some images we create in our dreams.

Early attachment behavior

Just as with auditory patterns, the newborn's brain is capable of processing a huge range of visual information in an attempt to make sense out of the initial chaos. It seems that not only are we pre-programmed to prefer human faces over similarly complex but less meaningless forms, but also to detect eye contact (Farroni *et al.* 2005), and even perhaps that there are sex differences in pattern preference, with one-day-old newborn girls preferring to look at human faces, while the boys preferred a mechanical mobile (Lutchmaya and Baron-Cohen 2002). Such early competence in visual pattern processing has implications for attachment, given that infants can and do quickly associate familiar visual arrays with primary reinforcement, such as food and physical comfort.

Understanding emotional cues

In terms of human interactions, we can see the look on someone's face that will clue us to his or her mood. Visual patterns indicate whether someone is mad at us or worried. We notice clenching of fists, aggressive body movements, and physical approaches that signal danger. The ability to recognize these patterns allows us to predict what is likely to happen, and thus to plan our own responses. In addition, we are able to respond nonverbally, with a hug or a shrug, knowing that providing visual cues to our own inner feelings is of great value to others. Thus, the ability to judge facial expressions, gestures, and other important body language is critical to the accurate interpretation of most nonverbal communication.

Mobility

Our ability to analyze visual patterns is critical in the acquisition of early mobility, and continues to be a vital part of our ability to find our way around. We know that visually impaired infants have comparable developmental motor milestones to their sighted peers up to the time they begin to crawl and walk, when they begin to fall behind. At home, I watch our beloved Labrador struggle with her mobility as her eyesight deteriorates, and the critical importance of being able to analyze visual patterns is painfully obvious. In our everyday life, the ability to see what is around us not only allows us to navigate around our environment, but to judge distance, personal space, the trajectories of others, and endless other aspects of making our way in the world purposefully and safely.

Safety

The analysis of patterns in our visual world enables us to discriminate the familiar from the unfamiliar by the use of an infinite range of visual cues. We can discriminate a friend from a stranger, know when we are at home rather than away, recognize a red traffic light, and see what the weather is like. If there is a change in the visual detail of our physical environment, we need to notice and interpret that change in order to determine whether it requires some action on our part. Being able to see that an approaching object is likely to intersect with our path and thus being able to take evasive action is clearly key to safety and survival. Just as it is important to recognize danger signals, it is equally important to recognize the familiar patterns of daily life that reduce our anxiety. Many individuals with visual patterning difficulties are highly anxious, in no small part because daily life requires constant analysis of a visual environment whose patterns are not immediately obvious, and therefore not immediately analyzed into "safe" versus "unsafe."

Implications for academic learning

Visual pattern recognition is basic to almost all aspects of learning. Most important is the acquisition of the visual symbols that represent language – letters and letter sequences that are critical to both reading and written expression. Children with NLD often continue to make reversal and sequencing errors, despite their competent reading skills. In addition, understanding of the relationships among numbers involves the ability to visualize number sets, quantity, distance, speed, functions, and so forth. In addition to visualizing patterns, math involves changing patterns by adding, subtracting, multiplying, and dividing them. The ability to read a clock face, and hence to understand the passage of time, is another aspect of math that involves visual-spatial patterning. The ability to recognize visual patterns is critical in many aspects of spelling, punctuation, penmanship, written math (e.g. +/− signs), and second language learning. Subjects such as geography involving maps, graphs, or diagrams may prove to be a challenge. In addition, good organizational skills often involve the use of visual patterns, color coding, charting, etc., along with the ability to present projects in a visually pleasing manner.

Gross motor patterns

This refers to our ability to use feedback from our skeleton and our large muscles in order to control such things as mobility, balance, and coordination. The importance of using both sides of our body in a cooperative manner is clear in everything from an infant learning to creep and crawl, to automatic functions such as walking, to an ability to play golf. Human motor development starts with an ability to control the trunk of the body, then the neck, then the four limbs, in what is known as proximal to distal progression.

Balance and coordination

Normally, our balance and coordination activities are laid down in the wiring of the brain as "whole" movements, rather than as a series of discrete little actions, and are so automatic that breaking them down or even simply thinking about them often makes us stumble and fall. Beyond the basic ability to walk and run, children (often relatively effortlessly) learn how to hop, skip, skate, ride a bicycle, swim, and do countless other activities that are important not simply for physical fitness, but also for leisure activities and social interactions. Children who are awkward or clumsy are at risk in many of these areas (see the section on Developmental Coordination Disorder for an in-depth look at this issue). Apart from the physical risk inherent in problems with balance and coordination, there are the social risks, perhaps more significant for boys, in the social "norms" for acceptability in an athletically oriented culture.

Self in space

The awareness of where the various parts of our body are is critical in understanding the whole concept of self in space. In order to find our way back from somewhere we came from, we not only have to recognize visual cues, but also our bodies need to remember, for example, whether we climbed up a hill, walked down stairs, turned several corners, and so on. We usually store such information quite unconsciously. We talk about someone having a "good sense of direction," and can tell from where we are not only where we have been, but also where we need to put ourselves next.

Team versus individual sports

Many individuals may have reasonable balance and coordination that enable them to engage in various athletic pursuits. While they may have few difficulties with individual sports (e.g. swimming, skating, skiing, biking, martial arts, etc.), they may flounder in team sports that require more pattern recognition skills. As Canadian icon, Wayne Gretzky, has said, proficiency in ice hockey depends not on being where the puck is, but being where it is going to be. The ability to "read" the play in such sports as soccer, basketball, volleyball, water polo, and so on, is critical to success. Being in the right place at the right time involves an understanding of gross motor patterns, speed of movement, and judgement of distance. An individual who is not able to do this will most likely not be happy in or chosen for teams.

Implications for academic learning

While gross motor difficulties may be the most obvious in physical education class, problems with clumsiness and coordination will also likely affect the acquisition of such fine motor skills as cutting, painting, and writing. A lack of confidence in physical competence can lead to low self-esteem which in turn can affect motivation and performance levels in potentially any subject area.

Fine motor patterns

Although clearly highly related to gross motor abilities, the fine motor systems function through a different system of pathways in the central nervous system, and are highly specialized. Not only are fine motor patterns important in terms of finger movements and handedness, but they are also critical in the coordination of the small muscles that affect speech.

Speech patterns

In order to articulate specific sounds in any language, there needs to be a high level of coordination among the various fine motor activities required of the mouth, lips, teeth, and tongue. The difference between the "s" and "th" sounds is a function of a small difference in tongue and teeth positions. Try it. Making a series of sounds (e.g. puh-tuh-kuh, or "spaghetti") is also depending on the correct sequencing of a complexity of small muscle movements. The ability to make the various sounds accurately, and to sequence them appropriately, is developmental in nature. In other words, these are skills that are extremely difficult for young children, but in which proficiency develops with age. For children who have difficulty recognizing, remembering, and reproducing articulation patterns, speech can be difficult to utilize and/or understand. While it is not particularly common, there are a number of children with NLD who have an early history of articulation difficulties, often with subsequent speech therapy. Also, some dysfluencies – e.g. stuttering, speaking too quickly, and stumbling over words ("cluttering"), etc. – are seen in some people with NLD. However, problems with speech mechanisms do not necessarily lead to NLD.

Pencil and paper skills

The complex development of our fine motor system allows us to use tools of all kinds, whether it be to cut, carve, shape, pluck, grasp, draw, or write. Being able to transpose visual symbols quickly and fluently onto paper or some other medium is a uniquely human communication skill which allows for the transfer of thought from one mind to another. Thus, the fine motor system is a crucial tool in the development of literacy, and in our ability to communicate what we know to other people. In order to write fluently, we need to store a multitude of small motor movements in a "gestalt" way, so that we reach the point where writing a given word is automatic. Most of us do not have to think about writing our own name, nor about most words with which we are very familiar. We can do so, in fact, with our eyes closed, relying only on our motor memory and utilizing our "mind's eye" to check accuracy. There are numerous connections in our central nervous systems that cross-check between our visual and fine motor systems, and it is believed that our visual and motor memories are located in very close proximity in our brains. Thus, information from our muscles (proprioceptive feedback) is important in terms of pattern recognition and memory, and is combined with our visual memory in order to enable us to write without actually copying. Individuals with NLD who have problems with fine motor skills are therefore at risk for written expressive difficulties, especially if they also have visual pattern recognition problems.

Handedness and laterality

The development of both fine and gross motor patterns depends very much on the brain's ability to coordinate both sides of the body. In general, the motor systems are under contralateral (opposite side) control – in other words, the left hemisphere essentially operates the right side of the body, and the right hemisphere the left side of the body – although there are many association pathways that enable us to coordinate the two. Because the brain tends to like to work from the midline of the body out towards the periphery, right-handed individuals are in a position of advantage when it comes to the conventions of writing from left to right, since this is a natural direction for them. Left-handers, on the other hand, need to overcome this innate "pattern" in order to produce the written symbols. There has been much research in the area of handedness/laterality and learning (see, for example, Molfese 1988), with the general conclusion that mixed laterality (especially hand, foot, eye, ear) is often related to learning problems.

Implications for academic learning

Most of the academic implications of fine motor patterning difficulties are discussed in the chapters on written expressive difficulties. Less obvious academic difficulties may result from the early articulation problems that can interfere with the acquisition of sound/symbol correspondence and affect early reading fluency. Reversals of letters and numbers may persist and interfere with written language and math, and fine motor fatigue may influence quality of output in all areas of academics. Organizational skills, especially in terms of written output, are also likely to be affected.

Behavior patterns

The analysis of human behavior patterns is complex and way beyond the scope of this guide. Thus, just a few aspects will be discussed here in order to provide an indication of the difficulties experienced by individuals with NLD.

Basic behavior patterns

In general, humans will work for reinforcement. If it pays off, we'll do it again. If we get nothing out of it, we won't bother. If we're punished for it, we may suppress the behavior, and punishment does not teach us new behaviors. Even fairly simple organisms work on these general principles, and, like the laboratory rat, we learn to turn left in the maze if there is food at the end of that passageway. If the pattern of reinforcement is consistent, we learn quickly. If the reinforcement is powerful enough, we keep doing the same thing over and over even if we are reinforced for it only once in a blue moon. This very simple paradigm is the building block for much more complex behaviors. Therefore, if an individual does not recognize or learn the basic pattern, there will be difficulties in all the more complex behaviors that are built on that basic pattern. Individuals with NLD are often reported to have difficulties following routines, even when they are exposed to them frequently, beyond what might be expected from a somewhat reluctant child. Consistency in the pattern of reinforcement is important for all children, but even more so for children with NLD. Parents and teachers who keep trying different ways of doing things may inadvertently be contributing to confusion.

Behavior "chains"

More complex behaviors (e.g. bedtime routines, getting dressed, homework, etc.) are made up of many discrete behaviors (e.g. brushing teeth, taking out a book, finding matching socks, etc.). Such complex behaviors are known as "chains" and often take on the same characteristics as more simple behaviors. In other words, they are stored as if they are one behavior. Once this happens, the chain becomes much more automatic, without the individual having to think of each single discrete behavior along the way. For individuals who do not recognize the chain of behaviors as a pattern, it is far more difficult to effect this type of storage and therefore the automatic aspect of the behavior chain is lost.

Understanding, prediction, control

Once we understand a behavior pattern, ours or someone else's, it helps us to predict what will happen to us or to others in a given situation. Even when situations vary somewhat, as most social contexts do, we often rely on what we did the last time as the best predictor of what to do next. Once we can predict a behavior pattern, we can begin to make choices about what to do to manage or control a situation. Given that individuals with NLD often experience great difficulty recognizing and understanding patterns of behavior, they are often unable to make good predictions with respect to what others might do, or what they themselves need to do. Thus, their behavior is often seen to be inappropriate, and sometimes seen to be making a bad situation worse. The difficulties understanding what is happening or why can lead to high levels of anxiety, frustration, and sometimes angry outbursts or withdrawal.

Self-awareness and self-advocacy

Individuals with NLD frequently have trouble understanding their own behavior patterns – how what they do affects others, how they tend to repeat behaviors that result in less than positive outcomes, and how others tend to react to them. In addition, self-advocacy is difficult when they attribute their problems to being "dumb" or "stupid," rather than being able to understand the pattern of their own strengths and weaknesses.

Implications for academic learning

One of the greatest problems for individuals who have difficulty learning appropriate behavior patterns is that these problems may mask or detract from genuine learning difficulties, especially when a child is "labeled" as having a behavior problem or identified with a behavior disorder. Following classroom routines, whether they be socially or academically oriented, is an important part of being accepted by peers and teachers alike, and can affect an individual's overall image. Teachers understandably become frustrated with children whose behavior requires energy to control, especially when it acts as a distraction or disturbance to other children in the classroom. The children, in turn, are frequently unavailable for learning because they fail to acquire appropriate learning behaviors such as good listening, waiting, focusing, and organizational skills.

Social patterns

If behavior patterns are complex, what can we say about social patterns? In our whole lifetime, it is rare to experience two social interactions that are identical, even between the same two people under identical circumstances. The nuances, reactions, emotions, chemistry, and a multitude of other subtle interactional issues ensure that each encounter remains unique, regardless of the degree of our preparation.

"Intelligent" social behavior

Successful social encounters tend to rely upon adaptability to the particular context within which they occur. Biologists define intelligent behavior as adapting to the environment by one of two processes: assimilation or accommodation. *Assimilation* is a process by which we recognize a new pattern as being similar enough to one that we already know that we are able to label them as the same. For example, a toddler may for a while call all males "Daddy" or every round object a "ball." We may respond to a new social situation by recognizing similarities to a previous situation, and therefore behave the same way we did before. *Accommodation* occurs once it is no longer helpful, or even working, to perceive everything as the same pattern, and so we accommodate by creating a new category of pattern. These "patterns" are then available to us for future assimilation. Once again, and by now to state the obvious, failure to recognize patterns significantly disturbs both our assimilation and accommodation processes.

Overt versus covert social patterns

In many circumstances, social patterns are open and can be described. For example, when you are introduced to someone, look them in the eye, hold out your hand, and say: "I'm John. Pleased to meet you." When you want to play with something that someone else has, ask them in a nice voice: "When you're done with that, please may I have a turn?" When you go to someone's house for dinner, remember to say "Thank you." However, in many others, there are no easy rules or patterns to follow. In such situations, we need to respond spontaneously, fly by the seat of our pants, and generally react with flexibility, by sensing what is required of us, often by reading someone else's nonverbal cues. Given that individuals with NLD have problems recognizing the most overt social patterns, it is easy to understand that more covert social expectations will prove to be even more difficult to detect and handle, especially since they are usually impossible to verbalize and "script."

Personal space and boundaries

Two key issues in social interactions are personal space and personal boundaries. In order to be successful in many relationships, we need to have a sense of social distance – how physically close we should be to others, for example, when standing in an elevator, choosing a seat on a bus or in a high school cafeteria, or when conversing with someone. There are no hard and fast rules about these; just a sense of what's right, gleaned from experiences of comfort levels and the reactions of others. We also need to have a sense of what is appropriate in terms of other people's privacy – not simply closing the bathroom door, but with respect to the type of questions we might ask and the kind of information we might disclose. We tolerate less personal space and fewer boundaries in more intimate relationships, whereas in casual acquaintances we tend to require more. For individuals who have difficulty recognizing these issues, many personal relationships are fraught with anxiety and failure, at least in terms of sustaining longer-term friendships and intimacy.

Friendship and relationship patterns

Given their excellent verbal abilities, many individuals with NLD, especially those who are less shy and more extroverted, have few problems in the initial stages of meeting other people. However, developing and maintaining the friendship or relationship present some challenges. When we are working on a new social relationship, we need to recognize the "dance" we are performing: the complex pattern of moves and counter-moves. How quickly we respond to an invitation and how soon we reciprocate will be important in establishing the intensity of the relationship. The deference with which we treat another person will indicate our perception of the social "hierarchy." The tone of voice with which we speak will reflect the balance of power in a relationship, especially those at school or in the workplace. If we are verbally aggressive or defensive, we are likely to alienate others. We usually learn these lessons the hard way by trial and many errors. But the patterns become part of the experience upon which we draw when it comes to each new relationship. The complexity of the ever-shifting dynamics of small groups – families, friends, classrooms, clubs, sports teams, work colleagues – defies classification, and requires flexibility, adaptability, and constant re-evaluation of action and reaction. The ability to recognize constantly changing social patterns in order to predict one's role in a dynamic involving others is something with which most of us struggle. For many individuals with NLD, it is an impenetrable jungle.

Implications for academic learning

Group learning situations are considered to be very important in most classrooms from kindergarten to high school. The ability to work as a partner or team member is a critical aspect of education, and one that carries through to all aspects of life beyond academics. Children who are unable or unwilling to cooperate with others, and who have difficulty sharing ideas, time, or effort, are likely to have problems with teamwork in any area of academics, but especially in classrooms relying on "discovery" learning. In fact, the "discovery" philosophy is not the best environment for children who have problems recognizing patterns and who do not experience the insight necessary for learning in this manner.

Finally...

A few years ago, there was a fad for pictures called "stereograms" made up of small colored pieces that initially looked like an abstract mosaic. However, if one stared at it the right way for long enough, a specific image of some kind would emerge. Those of us who never managed to see the image can have some empathy for individuals with pattern recognition deficits, and for how anxiety-provoking it is to have to work hard to make sense of a complex visual world day after day without ever really seeing the picture that others see.

Once we can identify the particular information processing channel within which an individual has difficulties with pattern recognition, we can predict the kinds of difficulties they may have in many different learning contexts. Plus, and perhaps more importantly, we can begin to explore different ways in which to teach the same pattern through other, alternative channels.

Chapter 5

INTRODUCTION TO SUBTYPES

Parents and others involved with individuals with nonverbal processing difficulties are frequently overwhelmed when faced with the complexities of information associated with the "syndrome" of nonverbal learning disabilities (NLD) presented, for example, by Rourke and colleagues (e.g. Rourke 1995). Much of the research requires a sophisticated understanding of neurology, neuroanatomy, neurophysiology, biochemistry, and neuropsychology even to be able to concentrate long enough to read through the articles or books. Even those of us familiar with the jargon and willing to try often find it very hard to apply the wealth of research findings to the realities of daily life. Translating information about certain kinds of neurons in given parts of the central nervous system into realistic suggestions for teachers is at best a challenge, and at worst an impossibility. In fact, much of the literature on NLD suffers from the same problem as individuals with NLD themselves – too many words, and not enough follow-through!

Previous efforts at identifying subtypes have focused on academically based notions: "arithmetic or mathematical subtype," "spelling subtype," "reading subtype" (e.g. Rourke 1978; Rourke and Conway 1998). This has resulted in a direction for research that has focused on matching children on certain simple academic tests (for example, the subtests of the Wide Range Achievement Test, still utilized although with norms now decades out of date) and then searching for different neuropsychological patterns that these subgroups of children have in common.

Since the early 1990s in our group practice, we have assessed thousands of individuals, both children and adults, hundreds of whom we have diagnosed with learning disabilities (LD). From a clinical point of view, it is extremely clear that, not only can we distinguish between those with language-based and those with nonverbal processing difficulties, we can also identify subgroups within the area of nonverbal LD that are based on the results of our assessment results in the broad sense (e.g. cognitive, speech-language, educational, sensorimotor, personality, etc.). From an individual's overall profile, we can look at the pattern of strengths and weaknesses, and predict with some reliability the types of academic, social, and behavioral issues they are likely to be experiencing – and why.

Based on this wealth of clinical experience, we have consistently identified four clinical subtypes of NLD, based on presenting problems and subsequently on the profile from a broad-based assessment – in other words, on the information processing pattern model discussed earlier in Chapter 3, and therefore, according to that approach, we do not begin by assuming specific areas of learning deficit. In fact, many individuals whose profiles are consistent with a NLD are initially referred for behavioral, social, and/or emotional difficulties, rather than overriding academic concerns.

These subtypes have been termed perceptual, social, written expressive, and attentional. While they have some general features in common and some children may show elements of more than one, we believe that these four presentations diverge sufficiently from each other in terms of differing underlying neuropsychological processes to warrant being termed "subtypes," and believe that further research can and will support this notion. In other words, it is believed that each of these subtypes represents an essentially different pattern of processing strengths and weaknesses, and hence each is likely to manifest itself in fairly predictable ways. These manifestations will be different for those evidenced by individuals with, say, visual perceptual and visual memory difficulties than for those individuals with visual-motor integration and/or fine motor problems. These issues will be presented in more detail in each of the subsequent chapters.

These subtypes may or may not have some neuropsychological, empirical, or research basis – to date, there has been no systematic investigation of this. Suffice it to say that most parents and educators, not to mention many other professionals who are involved with NLD children, become discouraged, and even depressed, when faced with the huge complexity and doom-and-gloom prognosis of the whole syndrome. We all need to be able to grasp what we are dealing with, and find a place to start. These subtypes allow us all to focus on clusters of symptoms and presenting issues which, in turn, encourages us to start somewhere, without being overwhelmed. Each subtype generates somewhat different sets of recommendations for educational, social, and behavioral management, which can help us take that first small step on the journey towards self-awareness, self-advocacy, and success that are the goals of our interventions.

As mentioned, these subtypes are often not mutually exclusive. There may well be some attention difficulties in addition to written expressive problems, or some mild social concerns in an individual with primarily visual pattern recognition weaknesses. Some individuals show evidence of all four. The advice to those living and working with NLD is to decide which of the symptoms or set of symptoms is currently causing the most interference with life – and start there. For a younger elementary school child, it may be the visual memory or attentional difficulties; for an adolescent or adult, it may be the social difficulties; for a youngster struggling with marks, it may be the written expressive problems.

There are also a number of childhood disorders that may present similar concerns, and there is currently much debate with respect to differential diagnoses among these various categories. The purpose of the subsequent chapters is not to resolve this debate, nor even to present each issue in detail. The following will simply introduce you to some other disorders (specifically Asperger's Syndrome, Developmental Coordination Disorder, and Attention Deficit Hyperactivity Disorder) that may be either associated with or confused with the various subtypes of NLD. In order for a competent differential diagnosis to be made, a full, often multidisciplinary, assessment is necessary. Nonetheless, the strategies outlined later in this guide can, and probably should, be applied, regardless of the specific diagnosis, if it is felt that the child is experiencing difficulties in some of the non-verbal areas.

In fact, even if there is no specific diagnosis, or in cases where there have been multiple, different diagnoses given over time or from different professionals, the advice is to pick up the ball and run with it. In other words, if an individual is experiencing a pattern of difficulties that is reflected in one of the subtypes, try some of the interventions to see if they work. With the exception of the potentially harmful effects of inappropriately prescribed medication, the remainder of the suggestions offered are benign, and it cannot hurt to try one or more. The degree of success of the intervention, however, may well differ, depending on the underlying cause of the problem.

While the four subsequent chapters outline in some detail the different profiles of each of the subtypes, Table 5.1 is a brief summary of the main characteristics.

Table 5.1 Summary of the main characteristics of the four subtypes of NLD

Usual presenting problems	Academic concerns	Strengths	Psychological process deficits
Perceptual subtype			
• organizational skills • time management • research projects • forest/trees issues	• mathematics (especially geometry, graphs, measurement) • geography, maps • visual aspects of language arts (letter reversals, spelling, organization on page)	• verbal abilities (vocabulary, verbal reasoning, general knowledge) • oral presentation • listening skills	• visual/spatial pattern recognition • visual attention • visual analysis and synthesis • visualization • nonverbal problem-solving • part–whole integration
Social subtype			
• social skills issues • communication skills • behavior • personal space • difficulty making and/or keeping friends • unaware of needs of others	• lack of participation in class • weak listening and reading comprehension • difficulty following instructions • problems working with others	• verbal abilities (vocabulary, general knowledge, grammar) • oral language • auditory learning	• behavioral/social pattern recognition • attention to socially relevant cues: visual (body language, facial expression) • auditory pattern recognition (tone, pitch, amplitude, timing, pacing) • social knowledge – absence/access
Written expressive subtype			
• behavior • anger management • low frustration tolerance • low self-esteem • "mouthy"	• quality and quantity of written work • task completion • homework issues • penmanship • spelling	• verbal abilities (vocabulary, verbal reasoning, general knowledge) • oral presentation • listening skills	• fine/gross motor pattern recognition • some visual pattern recognition • visual-motor integration • fine motor control • speed versus accuracy • visual memory • other psychomotor factors (laterality, self in space, directionality)

Table 5.1 continued

Usual presenting problems	Academic concerns	Strengths	Psychological process deficits
Attentional subtype			
• poor attention span • distractibility (internal and/or external) • off-task behavior • tunes out, daydreams	• problems with accuracy in math, written work • difficulty with written instructions • "careless" errors • incomplete work	• verbal abilities (vocabulary, verbal reasoning, general knowledge) • oral presentation • listening skills • auditory memory	• visual pattern recognition involving details • some behavior pattern recognition • visual attention and distractibility • tactile attention and distractibility • part–whole integration • speed/accuracy • self-regulation

Chapter 6

PERCEPTUAL NLD

Laura is a 15-year-old girl, brought for therapy by her parents for anger management issues. She is "freaking out" at home, screaming at family members to the point where everyone is walking around her on eggshells, and her younger brother rarely leaves his room. When she has a deadline looming – for a project, a test, an exam, a recital – she tends to leave everything until the last minute and then becomes highly agitated and demanding, to the point where she can be virtually hysterical. She is described as highly strung, anxious about many things, extremely bright, popular, gifted with language, and involved in many extra-curricular activities. Her room is messy and she lives in a whirlwind, and yet, at the same time, she is a perfectionist who becomes very frustrated when her world is not organized the way she wants it to be. Her parents report that she will frequently do her school work over and over until she is satisfied with the product – even if it means staying up late or getting up early, and even when they cannot see any problems with the way it was. She is struggling with her academic level Grade 10 math program and does not have many nice things to say about her teacher who, she complains, is an "idiot" who does not know how to teach. Her parents report, however, that she has had difficulties in math problem-solving as long as they can remember. Laura herself says that she is usually able to learn how to do a particular process (for example, solve quadratic equations), plug numbers into formulae, and remember "rules," but admits that she really does not understand what she is doing. Her teachers see her as a gifted, model student, with all her work completed neatly and handed in on time. She is a straight A student, except in math where she struggles to get Bs. She wants to be a doctor in a Third World country. Her assessment reveals superior verbal abilities, but very low average nonverbal pattern recognition and reproduction skills, and her visual memory is weak. There are no problems with processing speed, and she is highly focused. She is well-coordinated, and has no social skills difficulties.

Matthew is ten years old and struggling with his Grade 4 French Immersion curriculum. He works on his homework for many hours each night, with on-going support from both parents and a twice-weekly tutor. He had good marks throughout his primary grades, at least until the end of Grade 2. In Grade 3, he began to bring home much of the work he was supposed to complete in school, and his mother soon became aware that he really did not understand what he was doing. "Matthew just doesn't *get* it," is her frequent comment. His handwriting is reasonably neat, although it takes him a lot of effort, but he has great difficulty organizing his work, keeping his binders in order, remembering what he needs to bring with him for his homework, and knowing what he has to learn. He loves to read, especially comic books, and draws intricate pictures of battleships and rockets. While he manages to do reasonably well on class tests, he is having great difficulty with book reports, research projects, and other such assignments, and they are completed only with high levels of adult input, including tearing of hair and gnashing of teeth. His frustration with his school work is beginning to show at home; he is not sleeping well, and his parents are afraid he is becoming depressed. When Matthew's parents approach his teachers to request an assessment because they suspect he has learning problems, they are told that Matthew's oral work is excellent, and that his marks are still well within the average for his class, although everyone can see that he is struggling with math. There are a number of children who are a higher priority for the scarce assessment resources. A privately conducted assessment reveals a highly significant discrepancy between his high average verbal comprehension and low average perceptual reasoning abilities, along with weak visual recall, and evidence of problems with rotations and reversals when he is copying figures, letters, and numbers, which affects his processing speed. His auditory working memory and fine motor skills are all appropriate for his age. He is extremely well-behaved in school, excels at swimming and Tae Kwon Do, and is popular with his peers.

Characteristics

The primary area of difficulty for children with perceptual nonverbal learning disabilities (P-NLD) is that of *visual-spatial pattern recognition*. They usually present primarily with difficulties in general organizational skills, including: assignments unfinished and/or not submitted; messy and/or incomplete notebooks; missing notes, handouts, etc.; untidy binders, desks, lockers; poor time and project manage-ment skills, etc. They are more likely than their other NLD peers to present with some academic concerns, although these are often seen by teachers and parents to be the result of their difficulties organizing their work. These academic concerns generally focus on mathematics (especially measurement, shapes, geometry, problem-solving), visual (as opposed to rule-bound and phonetic) spelling, mapping skills, graphing, and task-completion. They frequently have comments on their report cards, or from parents, that reflect well-developed verbal abilities and therefore the expectation that they should be doing better in all academic areas. Some of these children experience problems with reversals and/or sequencing of letters and numbers that continue into Grades 2, 3, and even 4, reflecting their difficulty organizing and remembering visual arrays.

Commonly, they show major problems integrating parts and wholes – in other words, understanding that complex tasks can be broken down into small steps, and then that these steps can subsequently be followed in order to recreate the whole. This may relate to such widely diverse situations as coping with letters, words, sentences, and/or stories; keeping track of their daily or weekly schedule; or tidying their bedrooms. They become lost in the forest because of the trees, and do not always see that the trees are, in fact, part of the forest. They have difficulty with spatial and temporal relationships of all kinds, and therefore have trouble with mathematical concepts such as distance, speed, shape, three-dimensional objects, sets, and relationships among numbers (greater than/less than, n-times as many, divided into versus divided by, combinations, permutations, and so on).

P-NLD children show deficits primarily, and often exclusively, on tests measuring various aspects of perceptual organization, part–whole integration, and visual memory. They may show a relatively average ability to discern visual detail, but it is usually in the *interpretation* and *application* of this visual detail that they begin to show problems. Most often, although not always, they have great difficulties on puzzle-completion tasks (such as Object Assembly on the Weshsler Intelligence Scale for Children Third Edition (WISC-III)) which requires the child to make sense of a situation consisting of abstract and initially meaningless parts. Unlike tests requiring the sequencing of pictures to tell a story or follow a theme, in which a child can rely on language skills and social experiences, and on tasks where a model is available for comparison purposes, the child has to "create" the whole from visual images and/or long-term visual memory, while at the same time keeping track of the important details.

If their verbal skills are really strong, individuals with P-NLD may be able to use their verbal mediation to help themselves through nonverbal tasks, and so the scores on some tests may creep into the average range (especially if there is no time limit). If they do not appear to be using their verbal skills, they may go through a highly systematic trial-and-error approach, and it is obvious to observers that they are unable to visualize what something will look like until they have actually tried it. This approach is inefficient in terms of both time and effort, and is often excruciating to watch. This is where the experience of the assessor becomes important in noting the processing struggles that these children have on the way to producing an accurate final product.

There are some individuals in this category of NLD whose visual memory and pattern recognition difficulties appear to be specifically associated with the symbols of language – i.e. letters and numbers – and the important sequences of these that enable us to communicate by reading and writing. This condition is termed "dyslexia." This is a term used widely and freely as a general synonym for many learning difficulties. However, it does have a specific meaning, and caution needs to be exercised when using this label or diagnosing this particular disorder. It should be noted that dyslexia can result from many different underlying neurological mechanisms, including problems with sequencing, intersensory integration (especially visual/auditory), laterality issues, etc. It is therefore neither always possible nor helpful to distinguish dyslexia from either language or nonverbal learning difficulties, since it can be causally related to both.

Unless there are significant difficulties with the perception and interpretation of socially relevant cues, perhaps accompanied by other factors such as a high degree of introversion and social difficulties in the family, social deficits are not usually front and centre in P-NLD children. Provided they have been exposed to, and expected to follow, the rules of acceptable behavior at home and at school, they frequently seem to be able to compensate relatively well by using their linguistic competence and good auditory processing skills, enabling them to internalize and learn appropriate social interactions. Mitigating factors appear to be: a more extroverted personality; early identification of social deficits with appropriate social skills teaching and intervention; a highly socially oriented family environment where social appropriateness is valued and reinforced; and/or a high level of insight into the various requirements of social situations.

A note about organizational skills

It has been postulated that approximately half the world has a sense of order and likes to be organized, and half the world does not. Thus, while order, structure, and routine reduce anxiety in many of us, the rest of us prefer the comfortable familiarity of clutter. Individuals who are intrinsically organized revel in lists, routines, drills, structure, and, most of all, closure. Our brains are an automatic filing cabinet, with a place for everything and everything in its place. Clutter – physical or mental – brings anxiety. Decisions and choices are the bread-and-butter of the organized, and we cannot understand for the life of us why everyone else would not want to be organized. In fact, we believe it is our mission to assist everyone else to become organized. In this manner, our anxieties are minimized, and our world becomes quite predictable and ordered.

Children who have this intrinsic need for order, and yet who have difficulty recognizing the patterns they need in order to organize their information input and output, are obviously going to suffer great frustration and high anxiety. These are the children who will erase over and over again, because they sense the discomfort that comes with their efforts not satisfying their need to get things just right. Some of us can empathize because we have a similar need, and we know that our anxiety will remain high until we have a place for everything, and everything neatly in its place. Others of us will never understand why they simply cannot just let it be – it's good enough, leave it alone.

These others are from the remaining half of the world – those of us who are more flexible, with no intrinsic need for order; in fact, we see organization as rigid, uncreative, and stultifying. We value spontaneity and would much rather just "go with the flow." We are laid back and unhurried, unfazed by deadlines and relaxed about meeting them. We flexible individuals are not hung up on one way of doing things, and tend to be less judgemental about what is right and what is wrong. Order *increases*, rather than decreases, our anxiety. Why would we make a decision when another piece of information may well come along and change it? Might as well just sit on the fence, and wait and see. Lists, schedules, charts, and drills fill us with dread. Trying to make us see that organization is positive can be an uphill task, and can create much conflict and frustration in any relationship – parent–child, teacher–student, husband–wife, and so on. This is the case whether the helper is also a flexible type, in which case both parties are anxious about creating order for the same reasons, or whether the helper is an organized type, in which case both parties are anxious about creating order for *different* reasons.

There are, of course, times when each of us is in a state of disorganization, and most of us have at least one small part of our lives that remains messy. Those of us who are intrinsically in need of structure will be uncomfortable in that state, and will be motivated to move out of it as soon as we can. Those of us who are by nature more flexible and bothered by the rigidity of rules are unlikely to move voluntarily to a state of order. This reflects more of a personality trait, rather than a behavioral state. It is thus very helpful, and may even be essential, to understand not only the basic personality of the other individual, but also our own, before attempting to assist anyone with organizational skills.

If we are both flexible types, we will have a great deal of empathy and perhaps even more patience while attempting to teach someone with NLD how to be organized. This will be true, even if the person we are trying to teach is intrinsically willing. The problem is, we may not know how or see why. In this case, we need to understand that a certain amount of organization is necessary to survive in school, workplace, and life, and to look around for various models, programs, workshops, self-help books, etc., that can be our saviors. If we appoint or hire people (e.g. spouses or partners, teachers, tutors, etc.) to take over this role, it is sometimes hard for us to accept the perceived rigidity, and we have to be careful not to sabotage their efforts.

If we, as "teacher," are highly in favor of and competent at organizing, we are in danger of making the assumption that the recipient of our efforts is equally as invested. Because it is so hard for us to tolerate ambivalence, ambiguity, and indecision, we tend to become frustrated very easily with those who wallow in these states. The major pitfall is in our tendency to take over from those poor souls who have not yet seen the light, and to do their organizing for them. We are good at it; they are not. This very predictably results in our more laid-back "student" becoming even more laid-back – checking out even, and letting us do all the work. It is very important to recognize this tendency, and to remain focused on our job of helping the other person do this for himself or herself, even if at first he or she does not do it anywhere nearly as well as we can.

Thus, before we make a plan to help another person in the area of organizational skills, it is important that we are aware of our own "type" and preferences, since this will most definitely impact on our efficacy in assisting others. Then, if we can determine – perhaps by using the Student Styles Questionnaire (Oakland, Glutting and Horton 1996) or the Myers-Briggs Type Indicator (Myers and McCaulley 1985) – the "type" and preferences of the individual we are trying to teach, we are much more likely to be successful, and less likely to have a flat forehead from continually banging it on a wall. At the very least, we need to be aware that there are different strokes for different folks, and that life may not be as black-and-white (or as gray) as it seems from our own perspective.

Chapter 7

SOCIAL NLD

Melanie is referred at the end of Grade 3 because her parents are extremely concerned about some behavior problems at school, her lack of friends, and her tendency to be a "loner." Their anxiety is increased by recent news reports of school shootings by teenagers who apparently showed similar traits when they were younger. Mel is an only child whose father is a research physicist and a professor at a local university, spending most of his working life and his spare time in front of the computer. Her mother devotes herself to her daughter and is a permanent fixture at the school, volunteering for everything she can, so that she can keep an eye on her. She says that Mel does not seem to be able to handle the school-yard at all, frequently finding herself the victim of teasing or bullying, occasionally to the point where her mother or one of the teachers has had to rescue her. She seems to prefer adult company, or playing with children who are much younger. Her teachers are not worried about her academic progress, although her father feels that she is a very bright child who should be doing better than the bare average she is currently achieving on her report cards. However, the teachers are concerned that she is frequently off in her own world, and that they have difficulty establishing eye contact with her. They report that her behavior is unpredictable, and that her responses to them and to other children are sometimes quite inappropriate, specifically her tone of voice, or the degree of emotion shown. More often than not, however, she tries to avoid social interactions with the other students altogether. Both parents and teachers agree that she needs assistance. The principal is eager to have her diagnosed with Asperger's Syndrome, so that he will be able to access funding for an educational assistant to help both Mel and some other difficult students in the class.

Alex has been having social difficulties since he first went to playgroup as a toddler, being the first child ever to be expelled for aggressive behavior. He is now 11 and in a small private school, where the teachers have arranged for a "Circle of Friends" to help him socialize at recess times, since he used to be left out when the other children played. While he is never happier than when he has an adult audience to listen to minute details about the most recent science fiction movie he has seen, he does not seem to want to listen when others try to talk to him. He interrupts constantly, even in class, and does not seem to be able to modulate his voice appropriately, speaking quite loudly, even one-to-one in a quiet environment. His teachers describe him as "in your face," and unaware of personal space. He is quite a clumsy child, who is not particularly interested in athletic pursuits, but his family does not participate in sports, preferring instead to listen to music or engage in other arts-based activities. The family spends hours debating and discussing, listening to political commentaries on the radio, and reading. He has a much younger brother and sister with whom he is very close and protective, and he is responsible for the family's pet rabbit. Alex does not have significant academic problems, but his teachers say that he requires a great deal of input on their part to keep him on top of his work, and they have been making a number of allowances for him, since they have found his temper outbursts to be worth avoiding at all costs.

Characteristics

There are many children with nonverbal learning disabilitites (NLD) who present primarily with social skills problems and difficulties with interpersonal interactions – or, in pattern recognition terms, problems with recognizing both social and behavioral patterns. These may manifest as problems making or keeping friends; inappropriate social behaviors (e.g. "weird" behavior in the classroom, unsuitable conversation, etc.); lack of understanding of personal space, boundary, and privacy issues; difficulty maintaining social conversation (e.g. use of adult jargon with other children, inability to take turns in conversation, etc.); loner personality; fixation on certain topics or interests out of the normal range for their age group, and so on. Unless their behaviors are disruptive in the classroom, they are more commonly referred by concerned parents than by their teachers. These children are frequently being diagnosed with Asperger's Syndrome, particularly if they are not showing any obvious history of early language difficulties. It is felt to be very important to examine these children's cognitive profiles very carefully in order to distinguish social NLD (S-NLD) children from those who are more autistic-like, and/or from those whose social problems stem from environmental factors, such

as inappropriate or inconsistent parenting, chaotic family background, depriva-
tion, or other related social or behavioral factors.

Beyond the verbal/performance discrepancy, examination of the profile of
S-NLD children frequently reveals a low score on some of the perceptual organization tasks, specifically on subtests with more socially oriented themes (e.g.
sequencing pictures to tell stories, and completing puzzles, with the requirement
for observation of socially relevant detail), along with difficulties with tests
tapping social problem-solving. Some S-NLD children show a relatively low score
on tests of actual social knowledge – i.e. the "rules" and expectations of our social
environment. These S-NLD children do not only have difficulty reading social
cues, or nonverbal communication, from their visual environment, but they also
do not have a strong cache of internalized rules by which to monitor, plan, and
execute interpersonal interactions. In other words, they do not appear to have
learned how to behave in social situations either by being told what to do, or by
observation of other's behavior. However, many S-NLD children actually score
relatively well on tests of social knowledge, but do not appear to be able to *access*
these skills when required in real-life situations. This is typical of individuals with
NLD who may well be in possession of the specific tools, but who do not appear
to be able to access or utilize these tools in more complex situations because they
are unaware of the nonverbal cues – such as someone's tone of voice, facial
expression, body language, etc. – that would normally trigger a predictable behavioral response.

The inability to process and interpret visual cues from the environment is a
significant handicap in social interactions, albeit sometimes quite subtle. S-NLD
children may well be able to "talk the talk" but not always "walk the walk" in interpersonal situations. Because of their superb verbal abilities, they may often talk
their way into situations that they cannot actually handle. They may therefore have
little trouble initially making friends, but sustaining friendships proves to be very
difficult for them.

In addition to difficulties noticing, processing, and correctly interpreting
nonverbal cues from others, individuals with NLD frequently lack variety in their
own nonverbal behaviors, and are, in turn, hard to read when it comes to trying to
anticipate what they are thinking or feeling. This absence of social signals most
definitely has an impact on their relationships, in that most of us rely on many
factors other than words in order to judge someone's emotionality, sensitivity,
understanding, feelings, and level of involvement. Especially for those individuals
who are highly intuitive and sensitive to unspoken interactions, individuals with
NLD appear to be flat, apathetic, lacking empathy, or even quite unfeeling. Thus, it

is equally as important to tackle the issue of the projection of social cues as it is to help individuals with NLD read such cues from others.

There may be some gender-related issues at work when it comes to mitigating factors in the area of social deficits. S-NLD girls, in particular, appear to benefit from the female propensity for verbally focused interactions as the social focus, since their relative strengths in linguistic competence can sustain girls' social-rules-based play. Boys with S-NLD, however, may well suffer from difficulties in more athletically oriented social situations, particularly when team play is involved in terms of having to read a play in soccer or hockey, for example, or in other situations where gut instincts are important. Extroverted S-NLD children, regardless of gender, can often be successful in the initial stages of making friends, but have considerable difficulty sustaining relationships beyond the introductory level. Introverted children are more content to withdraw from interpersonal situations, independent of the presence of NLD, and it is hard to motivate them to change because of the discomfort precipitated by social interaction. The S-NLD further exacerbates this tendency.

Although not empirically tested, our clinical observations suggest that it is worthwhile to remediate the social skills deficits of S-NLD children, specifically by helping them to translate social problems into words, thus enabling them to utilize their stronger, verbally based problem-solving skills and to learn various rules that govern the more predictable social situations. Care does need to be taken to ensure that the words are not dissociated from the actions. In other words, *in situ* problem-solving is quite critical in order to avoid a situation where the child is quite able to "parrot" what to do, but is still unable to self-trigger from nonverbal cues that enable him or her to behave appropriately in a real social context. Thus, a group setting with similar age peers is more likely to be successful in remediating many social behaviors than any other setting where the child is in a one-on-one setting with an adult, since in the former context, the presence of relevant nonverbal cues is more probable.

Asperger's Syndrome

Asperger's Syndrome (AS), which is an autistic spectrum disorder, and NLD are often confused, with some authors and practitioners not differentiating at all, others perceiving them as different points along a continuum, and still others seeing them as different, albeit overlapping, disorders (e.g. Stewart 2002). Many research studies purporting to compare the two are unclear, at best, as to the criteria used to separate the two groups in the first place, often simply stating that one group consisted of individuals diagnosed with Asperger's Syndrome and the other of individuals diagnosed with NLD. To complicate the issue, there is no consensus on the criteria for a diagnosis of AS, although there is some common ground shared by all. The definitions most commonly found in research and clinical arenas are those of Gillberg and Gillberg (1989), Szatmari (1992), the *International Classification of Diseases and Disorders* (ICD-10, World Health Organization 1993) and the *Diagnostic and Statistical Manual (DSM-IV)* of the American Psychiatric Association (1994).

When one reads the detailed and varied criteria, it can be very easily seen how confusion occurs, even within the descriptors of AS. However, there is nothing within any of these definitions that indicates the presence of a significant discrepancy between an individual's verbal abilities and their nonverbal, visual-spatial, visual-motor or motor skills, such as that present in individuals with NLD. Table 7.1 summarizes the similarities and differences among these various definitions,

Table 7.1 Summary of the similarities and differences between
Asperger's Syndrome and social NLD

Presenting behavior	Asperger's Syndrome				Social NLD
	Gillberg	Szatmari	ICD-10	DSM-IV	
Difficulties interacting with peers	+/−	+/−*	+/−*	+/−*	+
Indifference to peer contacts	+/−	+/−*			
Failure to develop peer relationships		+/−	+/−	+/−	+/−
Socially/emotionally inappropriate behavior	+/−	+/−*		+/−*	+/−
Clumsy social approach		+/−		+/−*	+/−
Difficulties interpreting social cues	+/−		+/−*	+/−*	+/−
Lack of social reciprocity		+/−*	+/−	+/−	+/−
Difficulty sensing feelings of others	+/−*	+/−	+/−	+/−*	+/−
Indifference to feelings of others	+/−*	+/−	+/−	+/−*	
Lack of spontaneous sharing of enjoyment			+/−	+/−	
Narrow, exclusive, abnormal interests	+/−*		+/−	+/−	
Inflexible adherence to nonfunctional routines	+/−*		+/−	+/−	
Stereotypic motor mannerisms			+/−	+/−	

Table 7.1 continued

Presenting behavior	Asperger's Syndrome				
	Gillberg	Szatmari	ICD-10	DSM-IV	Social NLD
Persistent preoccupation with parts of objects			+/−	+/−*	
Delayed speech development	+/−				
Superficially competent expressive language	+/−				+/−
Formal pedantic language	+/−				+/−
Odd prosody, voice, inflection	+/−	+/−			+/−
Comprehension impairment/literal interpretation	+/−				+/−
Lack of cohesion, idiosyncratic use of words		+/−			
Repetitive speech patterns		+/−			
Non-communicative		+/−			
Clinically significant early language delays			−	−	
Over-talkative		+/−			+/−
Clinically significant cognitive delays			−	−	+
Limited use of gestures	+/−	+/−*	+/−	+/−	+/−
Clumsy/gauche body language	+/−		+/−*	+/−	+/−
Limited/inappropriate facial expression	+/−	+/−	+/−	+/−	+/−
Difficulty conveying emotion with face/eyes	+/−*	+/−		+/−*	+/−
Avoids looking at others/avoids eye contact		+/−	+/−	+/−	+/−
Poor performance on neurodevelopmental tests	+/−		+/−*		+/−
Social, occupational, educational impairments				+	+

* Implied (i.e. wording is not exactly the same, but the concept is similar).

+ Presence is necessary for diagnosis.

− Absence is necessary for diagnosis.

+/− One of a selection of alternatives necessary for diagnosis.

and compares them with the characteristics of NLD. These different sets of criteria do not require *all* presenting behaviors to be evident for a diagnosis to be made. Items in gray indicate those factors that seem to distinguish Asperger's in all its various forms from NLD.

The major similarity between the two is that both involve difficulties with social interaction and interpersonal skills, although as can be seen in the discussion of the different subtypes of NLD, these difficulties are not inevitable in individuals with NLD. When present, social difficulties in individuals with NLD are associated with more general, and objectively quantifiable, difficulties in perceiving visual cues, regardless of context, and more global problems with pattern recognition that affect the individual's ability to understand, predict, and respond appropriately in a range of social situations, especially when more spontaneous interpersonal interactions occur.

A major difference between AS and NLD is that AS is an *autistic spectrum*, pervasive developmental disorder, with chronically restricted repetitive and stereotyped patterns of behavior, interests, and activities, which are far beyond the narrow range of activities, social awkwardness, and slightly eccentric behaviors that are sometimes found in individuals with NLD. The tendencies of many autistic-like individuals not only to recognize patterns where many of the rest of us do not see them, but also to gravitate towards those patterns, is well recognized, and again distinguishes AS from NLD. *Asperger's Huh?* (Schnurr 1999) is an excellent resource, written for children and adolescents but also informative for adults, that describes very well what it is like to have AS, and illustrates some of the differences discussed in this chapter.

It is important to note that many rating scales commonly used in the diagnosis of Asperger's Syndrome do not differentiate between AS and NLD. It is also not unheard of for AS to be diagnosed based simply on one or two characteristics (e.g. poor eye contact and narrow range of interests), or a single checklist, in the absence of any psychological or neuropsychological evaluation.

Caution should always be exercised when a diagnosis of either Asperger's Syndrome (especially "mild" AS) or NLD is given *solely* based on an individual's difficulties with social skills and interpersonal interactions. While both disorders certainly may have this common element, and may indeed co-exist in some individuals, it is important that a full psychological assessment is conducted to determine whether there is an underlying learning disability profile that may well be affecting other, more subtle aspects of the individual's life, particularly in academic areas. In our clinical experience, the learning profiles of children with AS do not show the significant psychological process deficits that are found in children with NLD, *except for* those tests or subtests tapping social knowledge and/or awareness (e.g. Test of Problem Solving; Comprehension subtest of the Wechsler Preschool and Primary Scale of Intelligence Third Edition (WPPSI-III), Wechsler Intelligence Scale for Children (WISC-III), Fourth Edition (WISC-IV) and Weschsler Adult Intelligence Scale Third Edition (WAIS-III); Picture Arrangement subtest of the WISC-III and WAIS-III).

In the author's experience, one of the major clinical factors that seems to differentiate Asperger's children from S-NLD youngsters is found in the individual's ability and motivation to acquire social knowledge. By definition, autism comes from the Greek word *autos* which means "self" and reflects the autistic individual's predominantly inward focus and lack of interest in interacting with others. Children with S-NLD appear to benefit appreciably from social skills remediation, either in a one-on-one, pragmatic-language-based program if they are not deemed ready for group interactions, or in small group settings with opportunities for role play. In our own clinical experience, retesting of NLD children on measures of social knowledge following such remediation often indicates significant gains. Asperger's children, on the other hand, do not appear to learn as quickly, if at all, since the motivation to interact is quite often lacking, even in a one-on-one situation, and they tend not to show improvement on psychometric measures from pre- to post-testing following social skills training. While many parents insist that their Asperger's child is very motivated to interact, our experience has been that the diagnosis is likely to be in question, and that many of these supposed AS children, when competently assessed, show a cognitive profile of strengths and weaknesses that is consistent with a diagnosis of NLD. In addition, by definition, Asperger's children tend to show more autistic-like behavior, including some stereotypic behaviors, perseveration, self-absorption, fixation on certain objects or themes, and so on. These autistic-like behaviors are not present in S-NLD children beyond what would be expected for an introverted, shy, and passive learner.

A note about introverted children

It is vitally important to understand the difference between normal introversion and social deficits. Introversion is not, in and of itself, pathological, any more than extroversion is. Introverted children, quite normally, prefer to recharge their batteries alone, or perhaps with one or two others. They tend to develop deep interests in one or two areas, rather than a superficial knowledge of many. They tend to take a long time to make a real friend, and then may well be quite withdrawn if that friend leaves or lets them down. "Observation before participation" is their rule of thumb. Small talk and idle chatter do not come easily, and they frequently do not enjoy or benefit from group activities. Thus, if NLD is suspected, it is important to assess the child's personality, as well as their cognitive and learning profiles, in order to ensure that their social difficulties are not simply part of the (thankfully) very broad range of normal.

If social skills deficits are noted, appropriate social skills remediation for introverted children needs to be geared toward helping them be successful introverts – *not* toward turning them into extroverts. In other words, an introverted individual would normally make one or two friends at a time, perhaps taking a while to find a kindred spirit, and would be more likely to do so through being involved in an activity of some deep interest, which is likely to be something that is not faddish or mainstream (such as stamp collecting, history, statistics, etc.).

Table 7.2 is taken from the *Student Styles Questionnaire Manual* (Oakland, Glutting and Horton 1996). This manual, which accompanies a self-report questionnaire, is extremely helpful in understanding the differing needs of children with a range of personalities, and in providing a wide range of suggestions for children with different learning styles. It draws attention to some of the similarities between introverted children and children with so-called "social problems."

Table 7.2 Summary of the different learning styles of extroverts and introverts

Extroverts	Introverts
Characteristics	
About 65 percent of students prefer an extroverted style. They are likely to:	About 35 percent of students prefer an introverted style. They are likely to:
• display energy and enthusiasm	• enjoy and need solitude and private time
• draw energy from what is happening in their environment	• develop their ideas by thinking about them before discussing them
• feel more energetic after interacting with people	• feel more energetic and focused after spending time alone
• enjoy talking with and interacting with others	• respond slowly to environmental stimuli
• respond quickly – plunging in first and considering or analyzing later – and thus appear impulsive	• hesitate, be cautious, and think before acting
• understand and develop ideas by discussing them with others	• have a few close friends with whom they spend time
• express ideas, opinions, and feelings to others readily and often	• enjoy working alone
• have a wide variety of interests	• be reserved and somewhat difficult to get to know
• have many friends and be easy to get to know	• be slow to reveal feelings and opinions
• enjoy large and small groups and taking a public role	• be happy to listen without saying much
• be interested in activities that produce quick results	• prefer to think about and understand a concept before doing a hands-on assignment that applies it
• like to move from activity to activity and stay busy	• pay more attention to their own thoughts than to what is happening around them
• enjoy interruptions and distractions	• prefer individual or small group work to large group work
• not be silent much and be uncomfortable with silence	• want a space of their own where others do not intrude or handle their belongings without permission
• need compliments, affirmation, and encouragement from others	• have a few interests that they pursue in depth
• prefer talking to writing	

Continued on next page

Table 7.2 continued

Extroverts	Introverts
Social relationships	
Students who prefer an extroverted style generally enjoy interacting with their peers, teachers, and families. They like to work with others, who in turn feel comfortable with them. They are stimulated by the people and conditions in their environment. They tend to communicate easily with others and are usually perceived as approachable and friendly. They usually have many friends with whom they talk frequently. They share their ideas and opinions readily and may talk openly about very personal things. They are also very influenced by those around them and respond well to affirmation.	Students who prefer an introverted style tend to have a few close friends with whom they spend time. These students need less social contact than others, and their interactions with others tend to drain their energy. They need time alone and will enjoy being with others more if they have some necessary private time. They may not talk as much as those who prefer an extroverted style. Others may listen and give more weight to their opinions because what they say is often carefully thought out.

These students are somewhat retiring and unobtrusive, but they can be quite assertive when one of their deeply held beliefs is violated. This assertiveness may surprise others. Although these students may seem to lag behind socially, they may have good interpersonal skills that are best demonstrated with close friends and in small groups.

These students may be pressured by those who prefer an extroverted style to act more like the extroverted students. Unfortunately, introversion is often viewed negatively, and students who prefer an introverted style may be seen as uncooperative, unfriendly, and less intelligent than their extroverted peers. An understanding of different styles can help others see the valuable qualities these students possess. |
| **Classroom environment** | |
| Students who prefer an extroverted style enjoy having a place to do group work. They also like having an area for trial-and-error work and hands-on activities. They tend to enjoy noise, and activity that verges on chaos can be exciting to them. When they must work individually, they concentrate better if their area has few distractions and little noise. They enjoy a visually rich environment that has attractive bulletin boards, wall posters, colorful objects, and books with beautiful illustrations. | Students who prefer an introverted style enjoy having a retreat or quiet place in their classroom where they can work undisturbed. They enjoy having a space of their own and prefer that others do not go into their space without permission. They appreciate peace and lack of noise so that they can concentrate. They might even be allowed to bring ear plugs to school so that they can shut out a noisy environment. |

These students generally prefer performance tests or group presentations. They can handle surprises such as pop quizzes easily. They may do better on written tests if their answers can be relatively short. They need to check their work for careless errors caused by rushing through the test. Although they may prefer to be around others when taking tests and doing homework, they may do better when they work in a quiet place.

Classroom applications

Students who prefer an extroverted style learn best when they:

- work in large or small groups and discuss subjects with others, including teachers, who listen and respond to them
- are given hands-on assignments and the opportunity to talk as they work
- give presentations to the class or perform other tasks in the public eye (e.g. reading aloud) if they have the appropriate skills
- switch from one subject to another so they do not get bored
- complete a long assignment in stages so they do not get bored
- do a hands-on assignment before they are exposed to a concept or theory
- are allowed to try out their ideas and then modify them through a trial-and-error process
- are allowed to respond to a question with an answer that they develop and elaborate on as they speak

These students tend to prefer written tests over performance tests. They are able to concentrate on written tasks, including tests. They prefer that tests be announced ahead of time. They may need to manage their time so they can finish, because they prefer to work in depth.

Students who prefer an introverted style learn best when they:

- work on tasks alone
- do reading, writing, and research assignments
- are allowed privacy and time to think instead of being asked to stay busy
- are allowed to work with a *compatible* partner on assignments that are to be done in pairs
- can give class presentations after two or three other students have already presented or even several hours later or the next day
- are allowed enough uninterrupted time to respond
- are allowed to prepare in advance rather than perform extemporaneously
- have a schedule or syllabus so they know what is expected
- are complimented on their careful work and reflection
- are allowed to work in their own way without being pressured to act like extroverted students (e.g. do background research before interviewing)

Continued on next page

Table 7.2 continued

Extroverts	Introverts
Classroom applications continued	

Extroverts:

- receive frequent attention and commendation from the teacher
- are given choices; they want to feel that they have an impact on their environment and that their wishes are being considered.

These students are *less* likely to respond well to:

- lectures, unless they have frequent opportunity to ask questions and talk themselves
- work that they must complete alone
- complicated projects that take a long time to complete
- situations in which they are spectators rather than participants
- situations in which they must be silent for long periods of time
- situations in which they participate only minimally or in which their contribution is small.

Introverts:

- are allowed to work in a library or other quiet place
- are allowed to pursue an interest in depth
- are allowed to work in small groups of three or four, rather than six or more, when group work is assigned
- are allowed to be spectators rather than participants
- learn a concept before doing a hands-on assignment that illustrates the concept
- do individual work on computers or with other tools such as scientific instruments
- can do pencil-and-paper assignments, such as practicing spelling words.

These students are *less* likely to respond well to:

- a constant diet of group work
- assignments that only skim the surface of a subject in which they are interested
- oral reports and other public displays of their work
- chaotic, noisy groups
- suggestions that they go out and play with others when they are interested in reading or in some project of their own
- constant praise and compliments; can become suspicious of too many.

Chapter 8

WRITTEN EXPRESSIVE NLD

Sean's parents and teachers are all at their wit's end. He is in Grade 6, and has just been suspended from school for the third time for fighting in the yard. He says he punched the other boy because he laughed at Sean's spelling and called him a "retard." He constantly talks back to adults and is verbally aggressive with his older sister. His school work is rarely finished in class, and even minor amounts of homework cause World War III between him and his parents. His teachers complain constantly that the small portion of written work that is completed is virtually illegible, and that he spends a great deal of time sharpening pencils, losing notebooks, and going to the washroom. He acts out in class, and spends so much time in the principal's office that they are considering putting a plaque with his name on one of the chairs. He is believed by everyone to be a very smart young man, since he has a broad vocabulary and excellent expressive language skills, and won both the public speaking contest and the science fair the previous year. Therefore, his lack of production in class is frequently attributed to attitude, laziness, and/or oppositional behavior. "Sean needs to put more effort into his work" and "Sean is capable of far better quality work" are common remarks on his report cards. He has been told that, unless he pulls up his socks pretty swiftly, he will find himself repeating Grade 6, while all his friends go on to junior high school. His parents are becoming somewhat alarmed, not only in view of his increasing aggression, but also because he is showing many indications of very poor self-image. He calls himself a "loser," says he hates himself and everybody else, and has started to say that perhaps everyone would be better off if he weren't around. This prompts his parents to ask for help for his aggression, low self-esteem and possible depression.

Jackie, 14, has not been to school in three weeks. Her mom is frantic with worry, and fluctuates between being supportive and incensed. Her step-father says she just needs a firm hand and should be made to go back to school. Many of her problems are attributed by her mother to her missing her dad who has recently moved to a different city, drastically reducing his accessibility to Jackie and her older sister. They have taken her to their family physician who has diagnosed her with anxiety and mild depression, and placed her on medication. Jackie's mom feels very sorry for her, and has reduced expectations at home to virtually nothing so that she does not stress her daughter more than necessary. Exploration of Jackie's school history reveals long-standing problems handing in written assignments, along with poor spelling, messy handwriting, and inadequate note-taking. Her report cards contain many comments to the effect that she could do much better if only she tried harder, and that her written work does not reflect what the teachers suspect she actually knows. Whenever the demands for written work increase, Jackie's marks decrease relative to those of her classmates. She has frequently been absent on days when she has had tests, and has been complaining of headaches and stomach-aches for many years, particularly on Monday mornings. She has avoided being retained a grade because her mother has pleaded with the school on several occasions, arguing quite correctly, that Jackie really knows the work, but simply does not produce. At the moment, she is threatening to harm herself if her mom makes her go back to school.

Joel, six, was identified last year in senior kindergarten as "profoundly gifted" with verbal ability at the 99.9th percentile on the WPPSI-III. He is reading fluently at about a Grade 5 level, and is reportedly good with numbers. His expressive verbal ability is impressive, showing a broad vocabulary and manner more like that of an adult than of a child, and he has a tendency to dominate all conversation. His parents turn to acknowledge him whenever he starts to speak, and it is therefore very difficult for them (or us) to continue a conversation without a great deal of interruption. Closer inspection of his assessment results indicate that measures of visual-motor speed and accuracy were omitted from the pro-rated calculation of his nonverbal and overall scores because they were relatively low (actually, average for a child of his age), and including them would have meant that he would not meet criteria for inclusion in the enrichment program. In Grade 1, he is creating havoc each morning before school, screaming that he hates school, hates his teacher, and hates work. His parents are burned out with their efforts to persuade him to go each day, and are resorting to methods for getting him there with which they are uncomfortable. They have completely given up on trying to get him to do any homework, which consists solely of independent written work that he has not finished during the day. They had routinely been spending two hours each evening battling with tasks that his teacher says takes other children about ten minutes to complete. He actively avoids picking up a pencil, and when he does so, holds it with his whole hand, rather than the normal two- or three-point grip. He refuses to print and throws tantrums daily in the classroom when required to do so. Even though he is described as a perfectionist, he becomes extremely upset when his teacher or parents try to correct his pencil grip or to teach him strategies to make printing easier for him. He has recently started calling himself stupid and dumb, with his parent' reaction being to reinforce the fact that he is, in fact, very smart. They are seeking assistance with the decision as to whether to place him in the congregated class for the profoundly gifted, or whether to leave him in his regular classroom where he claims he is bored.

Characteristics

Children with written expressive difficulties (WE-NLD) form a large, distinct subgroup of nonverbal learning disabilities (NLD), and are sometimes referred to as having a Disorder of Written Expression (DSM-IV). Their problem is primarily with *output*, rather than input, or *production*, rather than learning *per se*. WE-NLD children do not have difficulties in the formulation of what they need to write (this would be a form of language processing and come under the language learning disabled (LLD) label), but rather have mechanical or technical problems getting information down on paper, despite high levels of linguistic ability. Specifically, when it comes to their cognitive profile, they show a significantly low score on tests measuring processing speed, often with an extremely low outlying score on any subtest requiring the written transposition of symbols. A number of practitioners and diagnosticians using the older Wechsler scales choose to pro-rate the Performance scale score by omitting the Coding subtest, or substituting the Mazes subtest, particularly in younger children. It is, however, felt to be important to let the results reflect the V/P split due to the low Coding subtest score, rather than to mask it, since this is frequently a significant indicator of other fine motor and visual-motor difficulties which need to be explored with further testing.

The obvious discrepancy in WE-NLD children between their oral skills and their written work usually becomes most noticeable at ages, or levels of school, where the demands for written output increase. However, when questioned, parents often confirm a dislike and active avoidance of coloring, copying, tracing, and/or printing readiness activities from an early age, which has sometimes passed relatively unnoticed in the presence of the child's strong language skills, often accompanied by a desire for and attraction to books. Thus, parents frequently reinforce and encourage the child's linguistic and literacy pursuits without worrying too much that they do not seem particularly interested in what some families see as simply play activities that have little apparent immediate relevance to overall learning. Parents are, for example, less likely to make a child do puzzles, or complete "dot-to-dot" pictures, than they are to oblige a child to read or be read to on a regular basis. Despite this active avoidance of many pencil-and-paper or other fine motor activities, some individuals with written expressive difficulties show a remarkable talent for creative drawing, especially when they can choose the subject rather than draw to order, and they often produce incredibly detailed works. This can lead adults to assume that they are just being "lazy" when it comes to written production. The issue appears to be that they have difficulty reproducing accurately from a model, whereas they can generate from within and just go with the flow. After a great deal of lack of success with school-type pencil-and-paper tasks, many children develop what can almost be described as a phobic reaction when pencils, crayons, pens, whatever, are placed in their hands.

On assessment, many WE-NLD children show evidence of a measurable lag in fine motor development, and some of them have already been seen by occupational therapists even before they enter the school system. Sometimes, however, the lag may be subtle and may not be developmentally or statistically significant, and yet it is often sufficient to interfere with the acquisition of printing or cursive ("joined up writing") skills. It may be especially noticeable in children who are in instructional programs (e.g. some Montessori or other private schools, some French-language schools) that require the use of cursive script from a very young age, since many children of five or six simply are not yet biologically ready to carry out these fine muscle exercises.

Individuals with NLD have a tendency to be extremely slow copying written material, whether from the board, an overhead, a book, another's notes, or from other sources, copying letter by letter, rather than "chunking" the material for ease of transfer. This may occur even in situations where they can quite competently read the material, because they cannot remember what the letters or words look like long enough to transfer them to paper. If they repeat the material verbally to themselves and have a reasonable auditory memory, this will often improve the situation slightly, although their spelling will then predictably deteriorate, since they are unable to recall the correct version of the words from their visual memory. If they are forced to go fast, they make many more errors and become frustrated and often ashamed of their work. Non-completion of assignments, or failing to hand in assignments that are in fact completed, is one of the most common signs of children who have written expressive difficulties. Feelings of embarrassment or shame result in children hiding assignments in their desk or schoolbag, or at home. The homework book often gets "lost" or forgotten. Parents often report that children worked hard on assignments, and are puzzled why they do not get handed in.

A number, but by no means the majority, of WE-NLD children are left-handed. Left-handers *consciously* have to overcome the brain's automatic tendency to move the hand from the midline of the body outwards, which for left-handers sends them from right to left. They therefore have to concentrate especially hard when learning to print and write, particularly when being taught by a right-handed teacher and watching right-handed peers. They may still be forming the letters consciously, when most of their classmates are doing so automatically. This detracts from their ability to concentrate on other aspects of the task (e.g. listening, following directions, understanding what they write, etc.).

For many WE-NLD children, letter and number reversals can be a chronic problem, especially with p/q, b/d, n/u, m/w, t/f, 2, s, z. Reversals are common in the early stages of printing and are not something to panic about, nor a sign that a child is dyslexic. Most children who make these errors are simply following their natural tendency to start writing by making a clockwise motion for right-handers and a counter-clockwise motion for left-handers. Thus, right-handed children make errors on, for example, c, s, 5, 6, while left-handed children make errors on z, 2, 3, 7, and so on. However, for *any* child who confuses the letter formations, or for those who have to check each one out to make sure it is correct, the additional effort required again detracts from what they are supposed to be focusing on and they often get left behind and become discouraged.

Spelling problems tend to be evident, both with sound/symbol correspondence during phonic exercises, and with sight words. It is often reported that these children have auditory problems because they do not seem to be learning by a phonic approach. Rather than being due to problems with phonological awareness, these difficulties are often due to a weak long-term visual memory for letter formations, and to an inability to reproduce them from the mind's eye onto paper. Careful assessment to determine what is visual and what is auditory processing problems is most useful, and can be teased out by the use of tests such as the Slingerland, the Woodcock-Johnson Tests of Cognitive Ability, the Detroit Test of Learning Ability, and so on.

Children with WE-NLD tend to simplify their thoughts when they put them on paper, in terms of both quality and quantity. They may be extremely economical in their use of vocabulary (will substitute the word "nice" for "beautiful," for example), even though you know they have a broad lexicon which they use well orally.

While WE-NLD children show few, if any, difficulties in math in the early grades, problems arise when the math becomes increasingly written, since they often have difficulty lining up the rows and columns, and hence make errors when writing that they do not make when they are manipulating the numbers in their heads. Some children are reported as having problems with reading comprehension. However, careful task analysis of tests purporting to measure reading comprehension frequently reveals that the mode of response is written, rather than oral, which confounds the issue of assessing a child's ability to understand what he or she reads.

Children with WE-NLD develop a potentially large repertoire of avoidance behaviors around written work, which, in addition to active refusal, could also include a compelling need to sharpen a pencil endlessly, chatting to other children, acting out behaviors resulting in removal from the classroom, crying, being "helpful" when it is not expected, defiance, trips to the bathroom, tummy-aches, headaches, and frequent absences from school. These children are often referred for "behavioral problems," or for signs of stress (bedwetting, somatic complaints, sleep disturbances, avoidance of school, etc.). It should be noted that not all avoidance behaviors are negative. Altruistic-type avoidance behaviors are frequently missed, and that many "helpful" and "sociable" children use these behaviors quite successfully for a long time before their difficulties with academics are noticed.

A significant number of WE-NLD children tend to be perceived as lazy and end up with comments on reports cards like: "does not complete his work in class," "is not working up to potential," "could do better with more effort," and so on. It is probably reasonable to assume that young children are not generally lazy. They do tend to avoid things that are difficult for them, just as we all do. This is not to say that there is no such thing as a lazy child. What is needed is some careful analysis of what the child seems to be avoiding and whether he or she has the necessary skills to complete that task.

Problems with written expression frequently translate into high levels of stress over homework. This constitutes a whole document of its own, since many children without problems, and their parents, become stressed over homework. However, parents often become aware of their child's difficulties with written expression when trying to get the work done. On occasion, at least one parent has had similar difficulties and fluctuates between sympathy and frustration. Often it transpires that one or both parents experienced great difficulty in school, and perhaps failed grades and/or dropped out because of non-recognition of this problem. This sometimes results in very high parental anxiety levels, and/or high expectations for the child, especially when they know he or she is bright.

One of the signs of a true written expressive disorder is that the individual has great difficulty improving his or her work, either in terms of accuracy or speed, even when offered attractive incentives or threatened with dire consequences. The question: "Under what circumstances *can* he go faster/be more accurate/produce neater work?" can often elicit the fact that he can, or he cannot. The question then becomes: "If he *can*, how do we *get* him to do it?" or "If he *can't*, how can we *help* him to do it?"

Occasionally, a WE-NLD child may become significantly discouraged, and even show a high level of acting out behavior, or some serious symptoms of depression. By the time things reach this stage, the child is often quite desperate, and the possibility of a learning disability has frequently not been suspected, let alone correctly identified or addressed. When professional input is sought for such behaviors, it is important to explore the possibility of some form of nonverbal learning difficulty, including a written expressive disorder, as one of the contributing factors. Early assessment and identification are critical in order to prevent secondary emotional disturbances.

A note about "internalized messages"

In these days of computer technology, video games, TV, keyboarding, and voice recognition software, there are many children who would simply prefer not to write. It is hard, it is routine, it involves lots of drills and practices – in a word, it's boring. Many children are growing up with the following messages:

- "I should never be bored. I should always be stimulated and challenged."

- "I should always be happy."

- "I should always be comfortable."

- "I should always be given a reason for everything I am asked to do. If I do not agree with the reason, I should not have to do what I am asked to do."

- "When life gets tough, opt out."

Many parents are under the impression that it is somehow mean or even "abusive" to make children do things that they are unwilling to do, especially if parents have bought into the idea that children need to be given reasons for every request. Most of us like to take the easy way if we possibly can, and most of us will do so, given half a chance. It is very important to distinguish between youngsters who simply would prefer not to write, and those who have genuine visual-motor difficulties. Children who can write reams about things that are of interest to them, or who can complete an assignment neatly and swiftly given a tempting carrot at the end, clearly do not qualify as WE-NLD. Once again, however, appropriate assessment of visual, fine motor, and visual-motor skills is the only way to determine whether there is a genuine underlying problem.

Working with internalized messages is frequently the purview of psychological service providers, and can be a complex process. It is hard to change, even when we want to. Having someone else comment that they think we have done a lousy job as a parent (or at least that is what we perceive them to be saying) does not always accomplish such changes. It is very important to create an atmosphere of cooperation between parents and educators if such issues are to be addressed.

These issues are dealt with in depth in *The Pampered Child Syndrome: How to Recognize It, How to Manage It and How to Avoid It* (Mamen 2006).

Developmental Coordination Disorder (DCD)

CONTRIBUTED BY CHERYL MISSIUNA, PH.D. AND O.T. REG. (ONT.) OCCUPATIONAL THERAPIST, SCHOOL OF REHABILITATION SCIENCE, MCMASTER UNIVERSITY, HAMILTON, ONTARIO, AND HEAD OF CANCHILD, AND DENISE DELAAT, OCCUPATIONAL THERAPIST, CHILDREN'S HOSPITAL OF EASTERN ONTARIO

Developmental Coordination Disorder (DCD) has been described in the past under a variety of labels such as the "clumsy child," "developmental dyspraxia", or the child with "sensory integrative dysfunction." In 1994, an International Consensus decision was held and researchers and clinicians agreed to use the American Psychiatric Association (APA) term "developmental coordination disorder" to recognize the daily movement issues that are experienced by many children (Polatajko, Fox and Missiuna 1995).

Children with DCD have normal intellectual abilities but experience problems with gross and/or fine motor skills that are not attributable to a general medical condition such as cerebral palsy, hemiplegia, muscular dystrophy, or Pervasive Developmental Disorder. To meet the diagnostic criteria for DCD, these *motor coordination difficulties must significantly interfere with academic activities or activities of daily living* (e.g. handwriting, self-care activities, and/or performance in sports) (APA 2000). Research suggests that DCD is a very common developmental disorder. In fact, it affects 5–6 percent of all school-aged children (APA 2000). The way that children's difficulties present, though, is really variable. Some children struggle more with fine motor activities, others with gross motor and/or balance tasks (Missiuna, Rivard and Bartlett 2003). The severity of the presentation is also on a continuum (Visser 2003) with some children managing to learn tasks with extra effort and others completely unable to perform daily activities such as turning a door knob, using utensils, or catching a ball.

DCD and other co-existing developmental problems

DCD can co-exist with a nonverbal learning disability. It may also co-exist with other developmental or learning problems such as Attention Deficit Hyperactivity Disorder (AD/HD), specific language impairment and other language-based learning disabilities (LLD) (Dewey *et al.* 2004). DCD can also occur as a "pure" motor disorder, without any learning disability, but the motor coordination difficulties may still lead to secondary problems with any academic activities that involve written output.

In the past, children's motor coordination issues were thought to be of minor importance because it was believed that they would outgrow their difficulties in adolescence. Researchers now have evidence that children with DCD are not likely to outgrow their clumsiness (Cantell and Kooistra 2002; Losse *et al.* 1991). It is not uncommon for the child with DCD to experience social isolation, bullying, anxiety, and depression as they struggle to perform everyday tasks (Chen and Cohn 2003; Hellgren, *et al.* 1994; Rasmussen and Gillberg 2000; Skinner and Piek 2001). Adults with DCD tell us that motor coordination difficulties are often not as much of a problem for them as the social and emotional distress that they experienced when they were children (Drew 2005). Understanding the child's motor difficulties, and accommodating for them, can make a lot of difference.

Description of the child with DCD

Children with DCD are often described by those around them as clumsy or "motor delayed." Although they usually achieve early motor milestones such as sitting and walking on time, they have difficulty learning new motor tasks such as skipping, hopping, or jumping. Printing, copying, cutting with scissors, and other fine motor tasks are very challenging. Tasks that are particularly difficult are those that require the use of two hands, such as zippers, buttons, shoelaces, pulling on socks, or throwing and catching a ball. Generally, children with DCD exert more effort or take more time to complete everyday activities. Because they often have low muscle tone, the child with DCD may have difficulty maintaining an upright position at a desk or at circle time/group discussion time. As a result, they seem to have a slouched posture, fatigue easily, and may lean on the desk, table, walls, or furniture for added support. Sometimes children with DCD look like they are squirming around because they have trouble sitting in a stable position.

Children with DCD initially try to keep up with other children but usually begin to avoid or withdraw from physical activities at an early age. They often have a profile of frequent injuries, reduced physical fitness, or may put on extra weight (Cairney *et al.* 2005; Poulsen and Ziviani 2004). Children with DCD should be encouraged to participate in physical activities in which they are likely to be more successful (Rivard and Missiuna 2004) and to develop other areas of strength (e.g. drama, music) that keep them involved socially and build self-esteem.

Some children with DCD have sensory issues and are either over- or under-responsive to various types of sensory information. These sensory issues can often be improved by making changes to the child's environment (e.g. cutting tags off shirts, tucking bed sheets in snugly at night) (Pollock 2006).

Identification of DCD

If you are wondering whether a child is demonstrating the characteristics of DCD, it is important to think about their daily activities such as the following.

- Where are the difficulties encountered (home, school, community, etc.)?

- Is the child having difficulties with self-care activities such as doing up buttons, using cutlery, or tying shoelaces?

- Are fine motor difficulties such as printing, cutting, copying, opening juice boxes, or completing puzzles difficult for the child?

- Are sports or active play activities difficult or avoided by the child?

- Does the child need to exert more effort when doing motor-based activities?

- Do parents or caregivers find themselves assisting the child with self-care activities, more than they believe they should?

- Does the child seem to be weak or tire more easily than other children?

Importance of identifying DCD

DCD is just beginning to be recognized by the health care and school systems. Generally, parents find that a diagnosis allows them to advocate more effectively for services in the school system through a focused Individual Educational Plan (IEP) (Missiuna et al. 2006). For example, if a significant motor impairment is present, handwriting may never become efficient. There may be a need for technology or adaptive equipment (keyboarding) or software to augment written output (e.g. voice activated systems). (For more information see Pollock and Missiuna 2005.) Another reason to identify DCD is that it often co-occurs with other learning disabilities (LD) and/or AD/HD. In the school system, LD and AD/HD may be recognized but accompanying motor difficulties are usually not noticed. If more than one difficulty is present, more than one diagnosis should be given (APA 2000) because the approaches used to remediate each one may be different (Martini, Heath and Missiuna 1999).

Only a medical doctor or a psychologist can give a child a diagnosis of DCD. However, occupational therapists (OT) and physiotherapists (PT) are usually the people who assess children's motor skills and ask parents and children about how much the motor skill delays are affecting daily task performance. OTs and PTs often assist physicians and psychologists by reporting on the degree of the motor coordination difficulties and impact on everyday activities.

Information about strategies for dealing with DCD is included in Chapter 14.

Chapter 9

ATTENTIONAL NLD

Andy is referred for assessment by his mother during his Grade 6 year at a private school. He has been experiencing some problems with his math, spelling, and written work, making numerous errors that he refuses to correct. He rarely finishes any assignment in class and hence has mountains of homework. He is described by his teachers as argumentative at best and obnoxious at worst. He is frequently out of his seat, disrupting others in the class, and uses every excuse he can find to be off task. Teacher ratings have him at significant levels on every scale except anxiety, and the teachers feel that his mother is simply in denial with respect to his behavior. They are completely convinced that he has an attention deficit disorder, and the principal has told his mother that, unless she has him placed on medication, he will have to leave the school. For her part, his mother sees Andy as being totally frustrated because he finds many aspects of his school work very hard. She spends up to three hours every evening struggling over homework with him and often finds herself trying to re-teach concepts or processes. Her ratings of his behavior are well within normal limits, and she claims that she sees none of the problems he apparently presents in the classroom. In addition, he is the star pupil at his karate class, and soccer teams are vying for him because of his excellent leadership and discipline on the field. His mother desperately wants to keep him in a school that has small class sizes, because she realizes that he needs extra monitoring and attention to ensure that his academic skills are kept up to standard. However, she is unwilling to request medication for a problem that she does not agree exists. Instead, she feels that the teachers simply do not understand Andy's learning problem. She is therefore requesting some psychological assessment to assist with a differential diagnosis.

Suzie is in Grade 4 and is described as "cute as a button," and a "social butterfly." While she's not considered a behavior problem, she tends to prefer to chat to her friends or sharpen her pencils, rather than to complete her work. She loves to bring a favorite toy to school and her teacher frequently has to remove it from her desk or her lap. She does not finish much work in the classroom. In fact, as soon as her teacher leaves her side, she stares out of the window, doodles on her books, turns around to see what her friends are doing, and starts thinking about what she is going to play at recess. When her teacher asks her: "Suzie, what did I just say?" she can usually repeat it exactly, and her oral assignments are usually well-presented, albeit somewhat spontaneous. Her written work is untidy and full of errors, and her teacher often finds unfinished work crumpled up at the very back of Suzie's desk or in the bottom of her backpack. When she does her work, she tends to rush through so that she can be finished first. Although formal testing shows that her decoding skills are above grade level, she frequently does not read written instructions accurately, and often has to start over, because she has answered a different question than the one asked. At home, there are constant battles and tantrums over homework, and her parents are exhausted getting the work finished and corrected before sending it back to school. They report that Suzie is an extremely picky eater, not liking foods that are crisp or crunchy, and that she will only wear certain articles of clothing because she is extremely sensitive to particular textures, tight-waisted skirts or pants, things around her neck, and labels on shirts or tops.

Characteristics

Many individuals with learning disabilities (LD) exhibit symptoms of attentional difficulties, most notably distractibility, short attention span, impulsivity, difficulties with self-regulation, excessive motor movement, poor working memory, tendency to daydream or tune out, and so on, sometimes accompanied by acting out behaviors. The relationship between Attention Deficit Hyperactivity Disorder (AD/HD) and LD is something of a chicken-and-egg phenomenon, in that a child who cannot focus, attend, and concentrate will have difficulties learning, and a child who has difficulties learning will frequently find it hard to focus, attend, and concentrate. It is well-known that there is overlap between these two disorders, with them co-existing in a significant proportion of children, and a differential diagnosis is often extremely difficult to make, even for experienced professionals. In addition, the wealth of information available over the Internet, often presented in the form of checklists of symptoms and signs, makes it deceptively simple for anyone and everyone to "diagnose" an attention deficit disorder.

However, upon close examination of the learning and behavioral profiles of children with NLD who present with attention difficulties (either inattentive or hyperactive-impulsive), it usually becomes obvious that they do not meet criteria for a diagnosis of AD/HD. Frequently, the "symptoms" are present only in school, with parents reliably reporting levels at home that are well within the normal range, and no problems in other settings such as team sports, group activities, or extracurricular events. Unlike most children with AD/HD, children with attentional nonverbal learning disabilities (A-NLD) generally have excellent listening skills, even when they do not appear to be paying attention. They can repeat what was said, and remember what they have heard to a high level of competence. They take in and store information readily when it is presented to them verbally, and can focus for long periods when engaged through their verbal and listening skills (e.g. being read to, debating, arguing a point, etc.). During individual assessment, these children do not normally show the distractibility, restlessness, and impulsivity normally in evidence with AD/HD children even in the one-to-one controlled setting, although they frequently lose focus on tasks that require visual, tactile, and/or fine motor skills, and when the materials presented are visually highly complex.

With the attentional type of NLD, the problems lie primarily in the areas of visual and tactile attention and distractibility. Inattentiveness and distractibility are two different concepts, with the former indicating difficulties attending to anything, and the latter reflecting problems because of attending to everything.

It is very hard for children with visual attention problems to deal with a visually complex world. They do not perceive the detail required to discriminate relevant patterns, and therefore have difficulty screening out irrelevant visual stimuli. In fact, they may spend lots of time attending to completely irrelevant visual (or other) aspects of tasks. Workbooks and texts that are deliberately designed to be colorful and complex in order to attract the attention of most people are thus a nightmare for individuals with visual attention difficulties. They cannot deal with busy pages of math, nor scan densely-presented material quickly to pick out relevant information, because visual scanning skills are often weak. Visual-motor and visual-perceptual tasks are often poorly performed because of very poor attention to visual detail. For example, misaligned puzzle pieces frequently go unnoticed, and minor details are missed when sequencing pictures to tell stories. Thus, the results of a cognitive assessment will often show a lower score on the index measuring perceptual reasoning, or even processing speed, than they do on the freedom from distractibility or working memory index that is usually significantly affected in children with attentional disorders. When asked to look over their work, they do so without noticing visual detail, and therefore produce many "careless" errors. The resulting minor mistakes in subject areas such as written arithmetic, written French, punctuation and spelling are often misinterpreted as attentional, rather than as problems with the detection of visual detail.

Problems with tactile attention and distractibility are often reported by and about individuals with A-NLD, usually from a very young age. We normally habituate to the overwhelming amount of information processed by our tactile system – the feeling of the air on our body, the sensations from our clothing, the texture of foods, the presence of saliva in our mouths, the pull of gravity, the surfaces of the thousands of items we touch in the course of a day. The central nervous system is attuned to these patterns, and usually only alerts us if there is a change of some significance. For children with NLD, there are often great difficulties tuning out this essentially irrelevant information, and therefore freeing them up to concentrate on more relevant issues. They are sometimes exquisitely sensitive to touch, and do not respond as other children do to normal physical contact. Many are highly aware of different consistencies of food – some preferring crunchy foods, some only willing to eat soft or mushy foods. It is often difficult for them to tune out such things as a creased sock or the label on the back of a T-shirt. Even as infants, they may become irritable in certain types of clothing – some reacting to garments that are too tight, others seeming to want to be wrapped firmly. Associated problems for some NLD children are hypersensitivity to bright lights or sounds that are perceived as loud, and so many of them have problems in noisy classrooms or elsewhere if there is too much stimulation going on at the same time. This has repercussions in environments where group activities are required.

In such circumstances, individuals with A-NLD will respond to the stress in their own intrinsic ways – either by "fight" (engaging in behaviors that are external, obvious, and intended to engage others), by "flight" (engaging in behaviors that take them away from the stressful situation, such as daydreaming), or by "freeze," which puts them in total shut-down mode.

Dr. Rourke maintains that children with NLD and attention problems tend to show symptoms of hyperactivity at young ages, followed by a middle childhood period of normal activity level, followed in adolescence by a tendency to be hypoactive (i.e. show below normal activity levels). See www.nldontheweb.org for a full discussion of this issue.

Attention Deficit Hyperactivity Disorder

Given the simplistic checklist approach that is openly available on the Internet as well as through many professionals such as GPs, counselors, and teachers, it is deceptively easy to make a "diagnosis" of AD/HD. It is therefore vitally important to know that there are other significant criteria that must be met in order to determine whether a diagnosis of AD/HD is appropriate. The symptoms of inattentiveness or hyperactivity/impulsivity are usually pervasive across the senses (e.g. visual, auditory, motor). In addition, they:

- must have persisted for a period of at least six months
- must be present prior to age seven
- must be evident in two or more settings (e.g. school/work and home)
- must cause significant impairment to social, academic, or occupational functioning
- do not occur exclusively during the course of a Pervasive Developmental Disorder, Schizophrenia, or other Psychotic Disorder and are not better accounted for by another mental disorder (e.g. Mood Disorder, Anxiety Disorder, Dissociative Disorder, or a Personality Disorder) (DSM-IV, APA 1994).

In other words, a child does not "acquire" an attention deficit disorder in Grade 3 or Grade 4, nor show it only in math class. Symptoms that are first noted at older ages or seen only in specific circumstances are thus more than likely secondary to NLD, language based learning difficulties (LLD), or some other causal factors. In addition, it is essential to be able to rule out the list of other disorders before focusing on a diagnosis of AD/HD. Thus, whoever is making the determination must be qualified to recognize the presence or absence of a wide range of alternative childhood disorders.

It should be noted, however, that many of the treatment approaches suited to AD/HD are also useful when dealing with some of the attentional aspects of LLD or NLD. Before a medical approach is tried, a definitive diagnosis needs to be made, behavioral measures instituted, and extremely close monitoring put in place.

Because the literature on AD/HD is so vast and to some degree so controversial, and because a thorough review is well beyond the scope of this guide, interested parties are directed to the following sources for a thorough description and resources:

- www.mentalhealth.com
- www.nimh.nih.gov/publicat/ADHD.cfm
- www.chadd.org

A note about active/passive learners

There is a need for children to interact *actively* with their learning environments so that they can experience their world by using their whole bodies, their fine motor systems, their visual-motor integration skills, their patterning abilities, and the living concepts of time, space, speed, distance, and varying animate and inanimate objects. Art and craft activities, playing musical instruments, and movement (such as sports, gymnastics, running, dance) are all ways of interacting actively, as are such pursuits as Lego, puzzles, large building blocks, climbing, swinging, and so on. It may not be immediately obvious, but these experiences are very useful foundations for the later understanding of a wide range of mathematical concepts, and for learning general organizational structures.

Many children with NLD are *passive* learners. They sit back and wait to be taught – like empty vessels waiting to be filled. This lack of interactive learning (e.g. asking questions, taking things apart to see how they work, following up on something they don't know by finding out about it, etc.) certainly seems to contribute to their deficits in acquired knowledge, and deprives them of opportunities to learn from experience. Many parents and teachers encourage passive learning by valuing children who are placid, quiet, and still, and who wait for information to be given to them. In fact, in many family and classroom situations, this is considered to be a great aspirational goal!

Some parents and teachers encourage active learning by providing discovery situations where children are expected to explore and find out about everything in their environment, learning what they need to learn as they go along. In such environments, children learn about going fast and going slowly; about climbing up and falling down; about different textures of materials; about making things and breaking things; about all kinds of three-dimensional experiences that underlie their understanding of sets, measurements, quantities, speed, time, distance, and so on.

It is important to note that, while many children benefit from discovery learning situations, many do not, and it is insufficient, and sometimes even wrong, to assume that a given child will learn simply by being given the opportunity to do so. NLD children, because of their difficulties seeing patterns, do not normally benefit from open-ended or self-directed learning situations. Their learning process needs to be monitored, especially those with A-NLD. Children who are constantly flitting from one situation to another, however, are variously labeled "distractible" – i.e. attend to everything – or "short attention span" – i.e. attend to nothing for very long. Similarly, children who ask endless questions are often seen as disruptive or annoying, and children who take things apart to see how they work may be called destructive. Adult tolerance levels for these behaviors may be high, in which case the children are seen as "kids just being kids" – or adult tolerance levels may be low, in which case they may be seen as potentially having AD/HD.

Being aware of the fine line between active learning and hyperactivity is, of course, always necessary. It is worth checking in with a pediatrician or psychologist if there are any concerns about the appropriateness of a child's activity levels, especially if they are interfering with any major aspect of life, such as behavior management at home or school, learning, social interactions, or family harmony.

Chapter 10

GENERAL APPROACHES
TO MANAGING NLD

One of the main reasons for describing different subtypes of nonverbal learning disabilities (NLD) is to enable us to customize recommendations for educational, behavioral, and social management. It is quite noticeable that, in the existing literature, no distinction is made between different subtypes and thus many of the suggestions made for remediation are not particularly relevant to different types of problem areas. There are, however, some rules of thumb that apply to remediating most types of NLD, and these will be addressed briefly, before providing some specific suggestions for the various problem areas in turn.

It is helpful for both teachers and parents to understand that it is not necessary to learn a set of specific new teaching or parenting strategies in order to meet the needs of children with NLD. Rather, it is important to recognize and identify with the types of problems experienced by these children, especially in terms of their pattern recognition difficulties, and then to apply common-sense ways of addressing them that draw from our own training, from previous experiences, and simply from knowledge of human nature in our daily interactions.

The strengths of individuals with nonverbal learning difficulties should always be borne in mind — noted, encouraged, and positively reinforced wherever possible. There is always the danger that the positives can be overlooked in our zeal to identify and remediate the weaknesses. The possession of an excellent vocabulary and fund of general knowledge, along with a strong listening memory and competent debating and negotiating skills, are all useful tools that can form the basis of lifelong learning and a fruitful career path. In addition, they can be constantly and effectively utilized as compensatory techniques to enable individuals with NLD to translate the world into a zone of comfort, where efficient problem-solving skills can be accessed.

It is worth repeating here that it is neither necessary nor ethical to wait for a definitive diagnosis of a NLD before initiating relevant interventions for children who are experiencing academic, socio-emotional, and/ or behavioral difficulties. If a particular approach or strategy seems relevant and likely to be useful, go for it.

Finding alternative input and output channels

Given the pattern recognition approach to understanding NLD, there is an immediate and obvious approach to managing it. If an individual is not able to recognize or produce patterns in one information processing modality or channel, try another. Check back to Chapter 4 on pattern recognition to run through the different options. If visual-spatial patterns are a problem, try talking them out so that language and auditory patterns can be substituted. If fine motor patterns cause difficulty, again they can be translated into verbal or visual patterns, or even gross motor patterns. In general, it is necessary to consider a multisensory, multi-input approach, along with alternative options for output where feasible.

Translating nonverbal into verbal

The primary key to remediating NLD is to make use of the children's areas of strength – most notably, their verbal abilities. This means essentially translating as much nonverbal input as possible into words. This approach includes the following.

- Labelling feelings and emotions, even if they appear obvious to others. For example: "I am starting to get cross with you," "That must be disappointing for you," "I am worried about…," "It looks as if that makes you happy," and so on.

- Talking aloud through printing, copying, and other similar tasks. "Up, down, up, down" will result in an M, while "down, up, down, up" will result in a W. "The red part goes in the corner" or "I need another blue piece to match the blue piece that's already there." "I'm looking for the one with the circle in the middle and the line along the top." "P – a – r – t – y spells party."

- Modeling self-talk while carrying out everyday activities in order to encourage task completion, error detection and memory for routines. This provides an effective means to show children that even adults constantly self-correct and redirect.

Encouraging individuals to read aloud, especially math questions or number sentences and instructions or test questions, accomplishes this crucial and basic translation. Putting everything into words enables the individual with NLD to access their broad range of problem-solving skills, to slow down, and to check for errors.

Bridging the verbal and the nonverbal

In order to prevent a complete dissociation between the NLD child's verbal and nonverbal abilities, it is important to connect the verbal with the nonverbal whenever possible. In other words, adults need to make an effort to catch the child in the act, so to speak. It is far more effective to label a feeling or describe an action when the child is still in the midst of the situation, rather than attempting to recreate it at a later date.

Avoiding over-verbalizing

Although tempting because of their overt facility with language, it is very important to avoid over-verbalizing to NLD children. This leads to the false impression that they have learned what has been said in such a way that they are able to perform the action. In fact, they frequently "learn" extraordinarily well to parrot, or even to paraphrase, what has been said, with no resulting change in behavior whatsoever. Over time, this may result in a widening discrepancy between verbal and nonverbal abilities, even further disrupting the balance that is required for competent performance in a variety of learning situations.

Learning in context

In view of their difficulty associating parts and wholes in integrative tasks or complex problem-solving, it is necessary to provide the overall context in which a particular bit of learning is relevant. Unless new knowledge is firmly anchored in familiar waters, it may well drift away. There is thus a danger in NLD children being taught skills out of context, in that they may well get to be very competent in that specific skill (for example, spelling by using word families), but may not use the skill outside the situation in which it was taught.

Sensory integration/multisensory learning

It is vital for NLD youngsters to utilize as many input channels as possible to process incoming information, and to learn how to integrate the information from all of these channels to optimize memory and learning. Occupational therapists are experts in the area of sensory integration, and can provide many suggestions with respect to maximizing multisensory learning. For the rest of us, it is important to utilize the see/say/hear trilogy as much as possible, with the touch/feel/smell senses also coming into play in some circumstances.

Patterning activities

The importance of patterning activities for all children, but especially youngsters who show many of the risk factors for NLD, cannot be emphasized enough. Dwindling resources and a vociferous call for a return to basics in education have contributed to less and less time being dedicated to such essential activities as music, art, and movement. While stringing beads in fixed color sequences, beating a tambourine to various rhythms, or learning simple dance movements might appear to be less than relevant to scholastic achievement, these activities are all vital in assisting children to understand and to recognize patterns in the apparent chaos of their nonverbal world.

General implications for teachers

Children with NLD learn differently and need to be taught differently – although it is not unlikely that other students will often benefit from the same strategies and approaches. With NLD students, it is important to remember that their language level is not the same as their communication level. They tend to interpret what they hear literally and often misinterpret information they hear or read. They may become sidetracked by an interesting detail and miss the main point of a lesson or of what they are reading. Their understanding needs to be monitored.

Asking these children to imagine or pretend may not produce favorable results, as these abilities may be foreign to them. They need more realistically based activities, while, at the same time, being encouraged to develop their imaginations and creativity. It is quite amazing how frequently we rely on others being able to picture situations in their heads, and how important it is to be fully aware of when we are doing so.

Some children whose motor skills are not well developed may have poor muscle tone and may find sitting at desks uncomfortable, especially sitting at desks to write. They may do better when allowed to kneel on the chair or stand, or move to another table when they need to write.

Multitasking is difficult for NLD children. They do best with routines and situations that are predictable, even though they themselves may not initially be able to recognize the patterns. Being consistent in our expectations is therefore important so that they can learn to predict. NLD children do not generalize well and have trouble integrating new information. They therefore tend to fall back on established patterns with which they are familiar, and can thus sometimes appear to be rigid in their thinking and behavior.

Practice, practice, practice

There is no question that learning anything new for most of us requires a lot of practice before we get it right. How many of us got into the driver's seat in the car for the very first time and knew exactly what to do? We start off being confused and quite inefficient. As we have more exposure and as we practice the various skills, over time we become more competent. We can measure progress by sensing that the task is not quite as difficult as it was a few days ago, and we are reinforced by these small steps. This applies to learning of all kinds.

In these days of multimedia entertainment, routine drill and practice are considered to be tedious and boring. Teachers and parents alike are actively trying to avoid being labeled as old-fashioned and are seduced by messages from advertisers and marketers that they require a plethora of toys, animated figures, gadgets, and software to provide a range of alternative learning options. It is quite clearly one of the messages of this guide that it is vitally important to tap more than one "learning channel" especially when one or more may not be functioning. However, when it comes to learning basic skills, we simply cannot ignore the benefits of practicing and rehearsing – whether that involves rote learning of facts, learning a song or poem, learning lines for a play, perfecting a golf or tennis stroke, or achieving different levels in swimming or skating. Practice is the basis of remediation, and needs to be part of a child's daily routine. Homework should be a major tool for practice – not for learning a new skill. Teachers who make children practice basic skills until they are over-learned and automatic should be patted on the back, and not classed as the staff dinosaur.

It is never safe to assume anything with individuals with NLD! Just because they seemed to know something yesterday does not mean they will know it today if the situation or setting is different. Just because they are in Grade 3, or 7, or out at work, does not mean they know how to use a planner, do basic math, play hockey, or understand the nuances of social interaction. Just because "everybody else does it" does not mean they noticed.

Chapter 11

STRATEGIES FOR ORGANIZATIONAL SKILLS

It has been discussed in Chapter 6 that approximately half the world seeks order, and half the world does not. Thus, while organization, structure, and routine reduce anxiety in many of us, the rest of us prefer the comfortable familiarity of clutter. It is thus quite helpful to understand not only the basic personality of the nonverbal learning disabled (NLD) individual, but also our own, before attempting to assist with organizational skills. The following suggestions are offered, therefore, with the preceding caveats in mind.

Different learning preferences

The *Student Styles Questionnaire* (Oakland *et al.* 1996) is a valuable instrument based on Jungian theories, and can be used to assess a child's preferences for being organized or flexible. The manual is also a goldmine of recommendations for children of many different personality types with respect to learning style. In addition, it is helpful for adults working with organizational skills training to consult any of the materials put out by the Consulting Psychologists Press with respect to the Myers-Briggs Type Indicator (e.g. Myers and McCaulley 1985).

Awareness of our own preferences

It is important for those of us who wish to help others with organizational skills to be aware of our *own* preferences, so that we can maximize the chances of our suggestions working and minimize the frustration involved.

- Adults who are flexible by personality may have an exceedingly difficult time teaching a child to be organized, unless the adult has successfully learned useful strategies that can be translated into child-manageable terms. Those adults who have been forced to become organized can sometimes be quite rigid about what strategies the child should learn. These adults may, however, be far more tolerant of the child's difficulties, and be able to understand how irritating imposed structure can be.

- An adult with a need for order, who encounters a child who does not share this goal, may lose patience very readily, and may simply not understand why the child cannot see how helpful organizational strategies can be. Sometimes those who are intrinsically organized do not exactly know how they do it, and may need to analyze quite carefully what their own strategies are before trying to teach them to others.

Fundamentals of organization

The basis of organizational skills lies in pattern recognition and reproduction. Without patterns, there is no way to organize. For individuals with NLD, organizational difficulties are often much more fundamental than color-coding or filing efficiently. It is unfortunately usually the case that NLD children actively avoid the very activities that will help them improve their organizational skills. Many nonverbal play activities assist children in understanding the combination of parts and whole that are intrinsic in the early acquisition of academic readiness skills. Many NLD children have great difficulty making sense of their basic, visual world. Thus, they need to learn the very simple essentials of organization that probably come quite easily to most other children, such as: matching colors; sorting objects by color, size, or shape; playing games that require visual matching (Snap, Go Fish, etc.); completing puzzles of any kind; engaging in patterning activities of any kind (stringing beads, building with colored blocks, etc.). Through such activities, they come to understand the basic principle that the same parts can be used to construct myriad different wholes, and that the whole can be broken down and reconstructed similarly or differently.

Encouraging active learning

It is important to encourage a certain amount of active and interactive learning, even if a child does not voluntarily choose to engage in such pursuits. The parents of children with NLD often report that their youngsters have always resisted three-dimensional play, art, and athletic endeavors, and that they do not enjoy these activities. It is hard to justify making your unwilling child engage in what is considered to be a play or fun activity. However, the offer of a preferred activity when the others are completed can often provide extrinsic reinforcement when intrinsic motivation is lacking. Setting aside a little time to do part of a puzzle before the child engages in a preferred activity (such as being read to, using the computer, or watching TV) can certainly become part of a daily routine. Keeping the activity time short can ensure that each session does not end in a temper tantrum – the child's or the adult's.

Puzzles to teach rules

Jigsaws or other puzzles that are accompanied by a picture model are excellent teaching devices for nonverbal problem-solving. It is possible to teach a child rules to follow that provide a generic template for multiple situations where a sensible whole needs to be made from initially meaningless pieces. Talking aloud is *vital* to assist a child in learning these rules. "Okay, first I'm going to find all four corner pieces and then see which one goes where. Then we'll find all the pieces with a straight edge so that we can make the frame." "I need a piece with a white corner and a little yellow on it." "Now we've done the outside, we need to find all the red pieces that make up the bus." If possible, it is very helpful to be able to leave the puzzle unfinished, to be continued at another time. This lets the child know that he or she does not have to start all over again, but can retain the parts that he or she knows are right.

Prompts, not directions

When teaching any kind of organizational strategy, prompts such as "Does that look right?" "Which piece do you need next?" or "What do you need to do next?" can be more helpful in encouraging the child to learn how to process the information, rather than the use of a direct statement such as "You have that upside down," "Put that one over here," or "Now you need a green square." Feeding back a question, rather than telling the child what to do, makes sure that the child is actively engaged in the process, rather than responding passively to direction.

Verbal explanations of nonverbal aids

Flow charts, mind maps, color coding, tables, and other visual mnemonic devices do not make intrinsic sense to those with NLD, and must be explained, *using words along with step-by-step demonstration*. Either one of these alone (i.e. verbal explanation or step-by-step demonstration), without simultaneous use of the other, will probably result in the particular strategy being neither retained nor used.

Using a planner

There are very few learning disabled (LD) children, whether language learning disabled (LLD) or NLD, who can manage without the ubiquitous planner. It is very important to remember that they are not born knowing how to use it just because one is provided for them every school year. It is therefore critical for teachers, especially, to recognize that children need to be *taught* to use a planner, monitored while they learn, and checked up on, even when they seem to have mastered it. Because of their difficulties making sense of their visual environment, they do not always notice what is written on the board, or posted on the bulletin board. Because of their written expressive difficulties, they sometimes make mistakes when they are copying, or do not get all the information down before it is erased. It is an investment of time to teach children to use planners, lists, schedules, calendars, etc. Teaching them to use different colored markers for different subjects, or types of assignment, or priorities, can be helpful. It may also be useful to have them pre-list subjects for the week, ahead of time, to reduce the amount they have to write down in class. They can omit subjects that usually do not have homework assignments.

Packing the backpack

The schoolbag is also something that children need to be taught how to pack and unpack. Making sure they have everything they need is something that they often delegate to parents or teachers. A list printed in large print on the back of the front door can be a reminder in the morning. It can start as a checklist (lunch, snacks, drinking box, pencil case, planner…) that the child simply has to follow. Once that is mastered, it can change to: "Do you have everything you need for: snack time, lunch, phys. ed., brownies…?" Then "Have you checked your schoolbag?" may suffice. As discussed later, the use of "I" statements can assist in transferring the responsibility for the activity to the child, rather than the onus remaining on the adult to ensure that reminders are given and activities carried out. This would be, for example, a list that says: "I packed my snack and my lunch," "I looked at the calendar to see if I have hockey today," "I remembered my things to take to Dad's house," "I put my homework in my bag," etc.

Work area

At school and at home, having a work area separate from a reading or playing area is ideal. This cues the NLD student as to what is expected when he or she is in this area. Any work area should be clear and uncluttered. Removing all unnecessary items before beginning to work cuts down on distractions. Physical movement from one area to another signals the boundary between the two, and provides non-verbal cues that hopefully trigger appropriate levels of concentration and relevant learning behaviors.

Setting up for work

Before beginning independent written work, it is important to ensure that the child is clear what work is expected, how much time has been allotted to the task, and what the consequences are for completing or not completing the task. It is helpful to ensure that the child demonstrates his understanding of what he is supposed to be doing, and does not simply tell you in words! Watch until he has shown that he knows what to do, and then leave him to do it.

Homework

An area dedicated for homework is the best approach. This area needs to be properly set up with all the supplies and materials the students will need. Providing boxes and file storage units for organization will help keep things neat. The homework area should be in a quiet part of the house away from activity and noise, and should not be in front of a window or in sight of the TV. It should be easily accessible by adults, but off limits to siblings. While many of us set up a wonderful "office" in a child's room, most children prefer to work where they are not completely isolated. If a child chooses to work away from others, it is important to monitor to ensure that the work is actually being done. If it is not, we need to pull in the reins and have the child work closer to us, until such time he or she can take the responsibility of truly independent work. A homework responsibility chart is included at the end of this chapter (p.119) as a starting point for dividing up the responsibilities.

Timelines and priorities

There is no substitute for good communication between teachers and parents, as well as between teachers and students, when it comes to homework. Agreeing on a set time for homework (usually defined as ten minutes per grade – e.g. 20 minutes for Grade 2, 90 minutes for Grade 9) is important, as is sticking to it, so that children learn how long the time feels. If the time limit is constantly extended and flexible, the NLD child will not learn how much work can be accomplished within a set period of time. It is important to teach a child how to set priorities (for example: red = work that has to be done by tomorrow, yellow = work that is required within the next little while, and green = work that needs to be thought about but not yet completed), and to help them learn that priorities often change, depending upon specific circumstances. Modeling this is very powerful, but something that many of us adults forget to do, or at least forget to verbalize and label it when we do.

Checking the agenda

As part of a homework routine, checking the agenda or planner is definitely important. However, it is also important for parents and teachers *not* to own the whole responsibility for this. NLD children are not born knowing how to use planners, so they must be taught, and reinforced for using it themselves. For any of us to use one, a planner must develop some intrinsic reinforcement of its own, and it may take some time before a child actually relies on the planner to be of use. It helps to put some positive, exciting things in the planner, not simply all the things the child would rather avoid. If the planner or agenda includes negative comments about the child's work or behavior, the child will lose it. So would you; so would I. If there is a need to set up a communication device between parents and teachers, find another way to do it. It is helpful to provide major subject area headings, such as "Math," "French," etc., ahead of time so that all the child has to do is to jot down the specifics of the assignment, especially for students with written expressive difficulties.

Teaching time management skills

Helping a child learn how to initiate and complete tasks, and to prioritize activities, does not begin or end with homework. It is vitally important for us, as parents, to expect our children to carry responsibilities at home that have the same underlying pattern as homework: knowing what is expected, how much there is to do, when it is expected to be done, how much time needs to be set aside, how quickly to work, how to determine what has to be done first, when it is being done properly, what has not been done properly and therefore needs to be redone, and so on. These issues apply equally to cleaning out the goldfish bowl, tidying a room, doing laundry, making a lunch, preparing for a birthday party, folding laundry, and so on. Children as young as two or three can be expected to *begin* to understand these concepts. By the age of six or seven, the underlying philosophies should be well established. We can teach a child to make lists, use the calendar on the fridge for "deadlines," cross off days on the calendar, and to make use of timers and clocks.

Telling the time

Many NLD children have great difficulty learning to use a traditional clock, and do not get a sense of the passing of time on a digital clock face. Although it is difficult for them, it is worth trying to teach a regular clock face, at first using words ("the big hand is at the top – this means…"), but also making use of colored quadrants, and teaching one concept at a time in the context of a particular activity. Most children who are desperate to watch a particular TV show will quickly learn the visual pattern of the clock face at that time, especially if the TV does not go on until they do.

Time versus speed

Just a reminder that giving someone longer to complete a set amount of work does not result in the individual working faster. Speed of working is an internal feeling – inner pacing – that needs to be experienced if we are to understand it. Having children practice beating the clock or trying for personal best times to beat their own record are ways to encourage such experiences. Expecting the same amount of work done in a shorter period of time, or expecting more work done in the same period of time, are both legitimate ways of encouraging any of us to speed up. Giving youngsters all the time they need while nagging them to go faster simply does not work. If, however, it is more important to get a task finished than it is to go fast, giving extra time is certainly worthwhile. Starting a child ahead of time, rather than having them always be last, can help self-esteem.

Encouraging independence

In general, there are issues around independence for NLD children. Since they frequently have problems getting organized to get somewhere or do something, adults tend to take over for them. When they are little, this is necessary. As they get older, it becomes quite inappropriate. Having your mom pack your bag for Cub or Brownie camp is quite different from having your mom pack your bag for your honeymoon. However, the transition from adult ownership to child ownership does not come instantaneously, and it is necessary to develop a way of handing over increasing portions of responsibility in a gradual manner. The analogy of a soccer game can help. As the adult, you may start out actually being on the field with your child, physically helping him to kick the ball, telling him where to stand, where to run, to whom to pass, making it easy for him to score a goal by stepping aside as he shoots. As he gets older and more proficient, you find yourself on the sideline shouting directions. Many parents get stuck at this point, wondering why the child does not think of what to do for himself. Low motivation, poor drive, passivity, and apathy are common complaints. For the child to take the ball himself down the field, decide where he should run, to whom he should pass, how to do his job, it is essential to let him try. He will not be very good at it at first – certainly nowhere nearly as good as the adult who has been coaching. However, he has to try. He still needs you there for support, but he needs to make his own mistakes, get up, dust off, and start again. His way of organizing may not be yours. He may have to learn some lessons the hard way. This is excruciating to watch, and you may still rescue on occasion. However, the old saying holds true. Give him a fish and he'll eat for a day. Teach him to fish and he'll eat for a lifetime.

Maps and directions

Finding their way around their environment can frequently be a challenge for NLD students, even somewhere that should be quite familiar. The "you are here" type maps do not seem to help, since the child sees his or her world from quite a different perspective, and cannot translate it to or from the overhead, bird's eye view. It is essential to walk the child physically through it, with verbal cues as necessary. "The math class is two doors past the water fountain." Try *not* to introduce any irrelevant information, such as "There's a red door on the left. Don't take that." He or she may do best with a student buddy or guide to help him or her, especially in a new environment such as a rotary system, or when he or she is quite young. Written instructions in the form of a list, like a recipe, can be helpful.

Music

For many individuals with NLD, involvement in music holds the key to understanding many nonverbal concepts, such as rhythm, patterns, pacing, harmony, and so on. Sadly, schools have been gradually dropping such activities from the curriculum. NLD children need to be able to do such things as: clap simple rhythms in time to music; anticipate what will come next in a musical series; recognize musical patterns; sing rounds or other songs where melody and rhythm need to be maintained despite competing sounds; learn poems, jingles, sayings, etc., off by heart so that they can concentrate on conveying emotion or mood, rather than just the words; act in plays so that they can learn to take turns; learn to perform on a musical instrument (recorder, xylophone, drum, tambourine – not necessarily anything more complicated); learn to play music in a group along with others, so they learn the need for tuning in to what others are doing, and the cooperative spirit in general.

Movement and fitness

Although all too frequently being dropped from the curriculum, movement, fitness, and athletic activities are extremely helpful to individuals with NLD. Learning to be aware of timing, balance, and speed are all critical to understanding one's nonverbal world. Judging how long something will take to do is a critical organizational skill, and fundamental to time and project management. Determining how far it is from here to there across a room, and maneuvering around objects in the environment to get there, are also critical to managing in a social milieu. Learning to be aware of his or her body and where it is in space can help a clumsy or awkward child be less so. For those NLD children who do not have problems with fine or gross motor skills, more value placed on kinesthetic intelligence can boost self-esteem and self-confidence. It can also provide a legitimate alternative for learning patterns.

Visual arts

The teaching of techniques in visual arts using color, texture, pattern, shape, perspective, and so on, is a critical option for encouraging general pattern recognition that can underlie organization skills. Art activities are, like physical fitness and music, frequently seen as frills, or rewards to be enjoyed after the real work is done. For a child to be able to paint a large red circle, then a small red circle, some learning has occurred. When the color of that circle is changed, or the shape becomes a triangle or a square, more pattern recognition has occurred. It is difficult for parents to force reluctant children to engage in art activities, which many NLD children actively avoid. However, making it part of the curriculum, and as such a "have to," will definitely be beneficial in encouraging everyone to take it seriously.

Homework responsibility chart

Task	Teacher(s)	Student	Parents
Teaching concepts necessary for homework	**		
Setting tasks for homework	**		
Ensuring students know what is required of them	**		
Deciding how much work is reasonable	**		
Determining how much time should be spent	**		
Establishing timelines for handing in work	**		
Finding out what homework has been assigned	*	**	
Writing homework assignments in agenda	*	**	
Taking responsibility for bringing homework home		**	
Providing access to the necessary materials	**		**
Collecting the necessary materials to do the work		**	
Setting up an appropriate place to work		**	**
Making homework a priority over other activities		**	**
Ensuring there are no interruptions during homework		**	**
Setting regular homework time		**	**
Checking in agenda to see what homework is required		**	
Prioritizing assignments	*	**	*
Doing the homework		**	
Checking over homework for mistakes/errors		**	
Identifying specific area(s) of difficulty		**	
Exploring resources to help with area(s) of difficulty		**	
Providing assistance to clarify directions/instructions	**		*
Re-teaching concepts if necessary	**		
Deciding whether homework is ready to hand in		**	
Handing homework in to teacher		**	
Evaluating quality of homework	**		
Providing consequences for inadequate homework	**		**

** Primary responsibility

* Can give assistance as required or requested

Chapter 12

STRATEGIES FOR COMMUNICATION SKILLS AND SOCIAL LANGUAGE

The following suggestions address the issue of communication skills and may be useful at home and in other socially based situations outside the home (e.g. school, with peers, in the workplace, etc.). In general, it needs to be borne in mind that children with nonverbal learning disabilities (NLD) do not automatically pick up those cues from their environment that guide social or interactive behavior. They must be taught directly and given opportunities to practice with familiar others, both children and adults. Speech-language pathologists can be of tremendous assistance in this domain, both for assessment and remediation of what are called pragmatic or social language skills.

Simple, concrete explanations and directions

It will be necessary to explain things very simply and concretely, even when you think that the child should know what you mean. This does not mean that you have to talk to him or her like a younger child, but rather that you use plain vocabulary and short, simple grammatical structures. Since he or she may have some difficulty with metaphors (e.g. "quick as a flash," "run like the wind", etc.), you may need to explain what you mean or eliminate them where possible if a quick direction is to be given or a clarification is required. We usually tend to add metaphors or analogies to help explain something a little abstract. With NLD children, it is necessary to do the opposite.

Positive job description

It will be very important to tell the child what you do want, and not what you don't want, since he or she requires a clear job description. This may extend to such simple directives as "Stay in your seat while you do your work," "Look at me when I am talking to you," "Listen to what I ask you to do," "Talk to yourself in a quiet voice," and so on, which other children have no difficulty understanding, sometimes without being told. It is especially important not to use double negatives, such as "I don't want you not to eat before you go." When we state what we want in positive terms, we then look for the positive behaviors and pay attention to them.

Closed-ended questions

Use of closed-ended questions will be helpful when specific information is required. "What…?", "where…?", "when…?", and "who…?" questions tend to fall into this category. "How…?" and "why…?" questions are open-ended and can be used when you are encouraging the child to tell you more about situations or experiences. When encouraging children to be more precise, closed-ended questions can often accomplish more than open-ended ones. It is important to be aware that closed-ended questions can sound like an interrogation, and may frequently limit a child's ability to think creatively. It is therefore important to be aware when we are leading and even controlling a dialogue so that we can choose to do so or not, depending on the purpose of the interaction. As adults, we often do not realize that we have switched to closed-ended questions, so we need to be alert to this. One clue is when the other person appears to have switched entirely to monosyllabic mode, although it has always been amazing to me how many adolescent boys seem to be able to hold entire conversations and make complex social arrangements this way, especially on the telephone ("Yo," "S'up?" "Yeah," "Nope," "Now?" "Kay," "Bye").

Age-appropriate versus adult jargon

A fine line needs to be drawn and trodden between exposing children to age-appropriate jargon and to adult jargon. Given that they may well pick up and retain some high level information that they appear to use reasonably appropriately, they will continue to benefit from exposure to normal language experiences, which includes adult conversational language. However, at the same time they may well be missing the more child-appropriate language required to play with their peers. Children's play has a jargon of its own that adults do not normally teach, but rather that children pick up for themselves. Other children do not always realize that they need to repeat or reword things, and a child who does not have appropriate child-language may be left out or actively rejected. Some sessions with a speech-language pathologist may be beneficial and/or language-oriented social skills group training may well be appropriate at some point, if this is available. The main issue is usually for parents to recognize that reinforcing adult-like conversation may well not accomplish their goal of ensuring that their child is accepted by his or her peer group. "How do you do?" may be appropriate for adults; "Yo!" is more likely to connect with other youngsters. While this is not to suggest that family values be tossed away, it does mean that we as parents sometimes have to swallow hard and allow children to pick up the current vernacular so that they can communicate with their classmates and potential friends. Yes, it may be superficial. No, it may not have literary value or substance. However, it is what connects children of the same age.

Teaching simple games

It will also be helpful if a youngster can learn to play some simple games with which other children are familiar. Simple board games requiring turn-taking and following simple instructions would be beneficial. Games of chance (e.g. Snakes and Ladders, Sorry! etc.) are preferable to games of skill if adults and children are to play on a level field. Card games such as Snap, Go Fish, and Crazy 8s can teach simple social interactive language as well as providing skills for interactive play. The book *Deal Me In* by Dr. Margie Golick (1988) contains a large number of games for children of all ages, classified by specific skills taught. Letting an NLD child make up his or her own game with its own rules is an enlightening exercise. This may give you insight into the child's understanding of the concepts of rules, fairness, and sharing.

Gross motor activities

Some children with NLD also have difficulty with some gross motor (large muscle) abilities. In this case, we may need to give them some actual direction and lots of practice with such basic skills as swinging on a swing, using a slide or a teeter-totter (seesaw), throwing and catching beanbags or balls, kicking a ball, even running or hopping – whatever basic skills they seem to be lacking. Again, they may not pick these up simply by observing. It would be beneficial to persevere with such games within the family, even if losing is not handled well. Familiar, comfortable adults need to provide opportunities for children to lose as well as win if they are to manage in the outside world. Siblings may be difficult to handle, but need to learn to be patient, take turns, help each other, and so on. Active parenting is required if siblings are being overly pushy, and certainly if they are becoming even remotely verbally or emotionally abusive. Similarly, active intervention by teachers is required in school circumstances where peers are behaving inappropriately. These children are unlikely to be able to rescue themselves. However, it will usually be more effective to stand behind the children and help them to handle the situation themselves than it will be to take over and do it for them. This requires direct instruction as to precisely what to say, accompanied by obvious presence and back-up where necessary.

Reading activities

When we are reading with a younger child, we need to be prepared to stick with simple books with lots of repetition, and to read the same material many times over. We can teach simple nursery rhymes and jingles, and encourage children to predict what comes next in poems, songs, and stories. In order to give them practice with more complex language, we can try using reading materials that provide metaphors, analogies, and humor at their level. *Curious George, Clifford*, and the *Berenstain Bears* series will all be helpful in that they tend to focus on common situations and problem-solving at the same time as providing the language and humor experiences. Dr. Seuss books captivate children with the bizarre drawings and rhythmic language, and they will learn some of the verses by heart. Books about favorite TV shows will also have some appeal for them, especially an older child. It is important that we read *with* them, rather than *to* them, making sure that they are active in the reading process. We can encourage them to comment on the pictures, using questions to help them to paraphrase what has happened so far and to anticipate what they think will happen next, so that they can associate the parts with the whole on a continuing basis. Even reading some comic strips with them will help in this regard – the language tends to be simple and the situations familiar and funny. Older children, in particular, will benefit from practice in paraphrasing the story line of books, TV shows, movies, and so on. Even commercials can be useful here!

Practice with key words

In order to help children understand what is going on and to respond appropriately, it is often necessary to have them practice picking out the key word or words that signal what is expected. For example, a "Why…?" question requires a "Because…" answer. This highlighting of key words or concepts will not only be useful in social situations, but also for oral or written questions in workbooks, tests, assignments, etc.

Turn-taking

It is helpful to give some specific signals when a child has given enough information and can stop. Many individuals with S-NLD, especially, do not have much of an idea of when enough is enough. A nonverbal signal (e.g. holding up a finger to one's lips) or single verbal prompt (e.g. "short!") can help. Turn-taking can be taught, not only this directly, but also by good modeling. In busy, noisy families, it is often the more extroverted children or adults who hog the spotlight, while the more introverted tend to sit back and let this happen. The tendency we have to over-verbalize to NLD children does not always provide a good example of reciprocal conversation! We also need to practice being succinct and taking turns in conversations. In a therapeutic situation, we can often use an object, such as a ball or a small toy, to pass to the person whose turn it is to speak. This does not work well in a more natural setting, but if necessary can be used temporarily, say at a mealtime, until everyone gets the idea.

Eye contact

One behavior that is of concern is eye contact, and many people get very agitated when a child does not make eye contact, because that is one of the diagnostic criteria for some autistic-like disorders. While eye contact is certainly important in natural conversation, it needs to be borne in mind that holding someone's gaze too long is not particularly appropriate, and that, in fact, periodic eye contact, or eye contact with some breaks, is usually considered to be the norm. There are definite cultural differences in terms of the appropriateness of eye contact, since it can reflect power differentials, gender role expectations, and so on. Whether we agree with these or not, or whether they match our own cultural expectations or not, it is necessary to recognize, acknowledge, and respect these differences. In our practice, we have dealt with many children who were simply not aware that eye contact is expected under certain circumstances, and we have learned to check this out early in the process of intervention. As parents, we need to be aware of what we are modeling, and what we expect in common social situations at home, such as greeting each other, giving or receiving information, conversing over a meal, saying please or thank you, and so on. One of the most powerful ways to get another person to look at us when we are speaking is actually to stop talking mid-sentence. "Please look at me" is a phrase universally used at some time or other by the parents of the world, and most of us have taken a child's (if not a partner's!) chin in our hands and turned it towards us. As with other behaviors that we wish to establish, the expectation that the behavior will occur, and the reinforcement of it when it does, are both necessary, and need to be consistent. Waiting for the child to comply often requires a silent pause – and sometimes we are simply too impatient.

Many shy and/or introverted individuals are uncomfortable with direct eyeball-to-eyeball contact, at least for extended periods of time. If we can sit side-by-side, for example in a car or on a couch while watching TV, we are provided with a socially acceptable way of not making eye contact while communicating, and at the same time are likely to increase the probability of a response.

Chapter 13

STRATEGIES FOR PROCESSING SOCIAL CUES

In view of difficulties with processing some nonverbal, socially based information, the following suggestions may help. In general, they all involve translating the nonverbal into the verbal so that the child with nonverbal learning disability (NLD) can process information in their stronger modality. However, do *not* over-verbalize. Be succinct.

Direct verbal labeling of behavior

Since the NLD child does not necessarily recognize visual, nonverbal cues as to how to behave appropriately, she will benefit from verbal labeling of her behavior, along with a directive as to what is expected. Examples of labeling behavior would be: "Jesse, you are out of your seat," "You are sitting there doing nothing while all the others are getting their coats on," "You are talking too loudly," and so on. Unless her behavior is first *labeled*, she will not necessarily follow a subsequent instruction. Just saying "Please go back and sit down" may work, but it will not hook her up with the visual cues and context that let her know she was out of her seat in the first place. This is a necessary insight if she is to police her own behavior, rather than always waiting to be told what to do. So, while it may seem very obvious, it will help her to say "Jesse, you are out of your seat. Please go back and sit down." Again, it is necessary to emphasize that she must be told what is expected, and not what is not.

Watching TV

Sometimes it can be enlightening for a child to watch TV with the volume muted. In this way, we can encourage them to process all of the nonverbal cues to what is going on. It may be frustrating for them at first, and they may try to resist. However, there are few children who would pass up the opportunity to watch an extra show – even if the privilege is contingent upon muting the sound!

Paraphrasing and visualizing

Having her paraphrase what she is to do will provide another means by which she can hook up the verbal with the nonverbal. "Jesse, what did I just ask you to do?" may elicit a straight repetition, in which case we cannot be sure she has processed the information in direct connection with her behavior. We may specifically need to encourage her to say it in her own words. We can encourage her to close her eyes and visualize what we are asking her to do, so that she can create a visual image that she may be able to remember and follow along with the words. "Go upstairs and get your red sweater" is an example of an instruction that would be amenable to this approach. For a younger child, the visualization may well be beyond her capabilities, but it can be useful as she gets older, and we are training ourselves in the meantime.

Teaching basic manners

Specifically teaching socially appropriate behaviors and when to use them will continue to be necessary, since children may not always pick them up by exposure. This includes the need to say "Please" and "Thank you," "I'm fine, thank you," "Excuse me please," and so on. In addition, it is necessary to teach them to hold open doors for others, to eat with their mouth closed, not to speak with a full mouth, and so on – much in the same way as is needed for all children, just a little more consistently and probably more frequently.

Transferring responsibility

There comes a point when telling the child what to do needs to change to asking the child what needs to be done. "When you have finished your snack, what are you supposed to do with your cup?" will set her in motion to process previously taught behavior. If we continue to tell her "Put your cup on the tray," she may specifically wait for this cue before doing what she is supposed to do. This not only increases adult-dependency, it also restricts her ownership of her own behaviors, and we are firmly chained into the loop.

Labeling feelings

Given that she will probably have some difficulty picking up cues as to how people are feeling, it will be helpful to label feelings so that she can learn to associate words with her own body messages, as well as with the reactions of others. "When you take Jeffrey's toy away like that, he gets very upset. Can you see the expression on his face?" "I know you are angry when you scream like that," "Jesse, I get angry when you… Please would you…instead," "I am disappointed because…" "I'm very happy that…" "My feelings are hurt because…" "It feels really good when you …," and so on. Encouraging children to "look at my face" will also alert them to the fact that we are expressing our feelings in ways other than words.

Modeling nonverbal social behaviors

It is extremely important to use good body language ourselves. Sometimes we, as adults, are hard to read. We need to make sure our body language is clear and expressive, and that it matches our feelings and our words. When we are angry, we need to sound angry and look angry – although, of course, we don't have to go overboard with this. When we are pleased, our body language needs to reflect this. In other words, our children should not have to deal with a double message that comes from apparently contradictory words and pictures.

There are many excellent additional suggestions with respect to social interactions contained in the books by Tony Attwood (2007) and Kathryn Stewart (2002) listed in the References section at the end of the book. Techniques that are suggested for children with Asperger's Syndrome and even with autism are often helpful for children with NLD, and may actually be more successful.

Chapter 14

STRATEGIES FOR WRITTEN EXPRESSION

There are two main purposes in intervening with individuals who have problems with written expression or, in fact, any learning difficulty:

- *to remediate:* to do whatever we can to find ways to encourage the child to practice and improve skill levels, and therefore to improve pattern recognition and reproduction

- *to compensate:* to find ways around the areas of difficulty by utilizing alternative means of output.

As a general rule, it sometimes helps a great deal to think of these youngsters as having a problem with their hands, as if they had broken a wrist and were in a cast. This enables us to conceptualize their difficulties in rather concrete terms and to be creative when it comes to determining compensatory strategies.

Because this is an "invisible" handicap, there is often great resistance to treating these children differently from others in the class if particular consideration is given to these students. Consider whether we would place a cast on everyone if one child's arm were broken. We need to have the courage to take the leadership role by telling the other children that it is basically not their place to be concerned and "life is indeed not fair." It is a valuable lesson for them all to learn.

It is important to distinguish between children who *cannot* write and children who choose not to write. These suggestions are for the former.

Many teachers and parents become overwhelmed by a lengthy list of recommendations, and either try to do everything that has been suggested, or become discouraged and give up. This is not meant to be a "to do" list, but rather a range of options that can be browsed in order to find some places to start, or to tackle the child's most debilitating difficulties first.

Assisting a child with a written expressive disorder usually involves a mindset change, and a positive attitude, rather than the acquisition of new teaching skills or the investment of a great deal of time. However, it is critical to remember that handwriting, whether printing or cursive script, is a skill that needs to be taught and practiced. We are not born knowing how to do it, and learning it is not a hit-and-run. The more we do it, the better we become. Yes, practice and routine may be boring. No, teaching is not a popularity contest.

Commenting on written work

Children with written expressive difficulties are often extremely sensitive about their difficulties, even if they have been quite obnoxious in their acting out avoidance behaviors. It is therefore extremely important not to point out their problems to the rest of the class, comment on their work in front of others, or to single them out or put them down in any way. If you do need to comment, please try to be constructive and positive, letting them know whenever you notice any small improvement in effort or product.

Evaluating written work

It is devastating for most children to have their work marked by other children in the class, especially if they have spelling difficulties, since some other children, and unfortunately also some adults, will often delight in "bringing down" a child who otherwise appears to be smart. It may indeed be necessary completely to abandon peer-marking if you have even just one of these children in your class. In fact, there are not too many good psychological arguments to be made in favor of peer-marking or peer-evaluation at all!

Avoidance of humiliation

Never, ever, under any circumstances, rip up or throw in the garbage any piece of work done by *any* child, in front of the class, in front of the child, or in front of anyone else, however angry or frustrated you may be. This is tantamount to emotional abuse. The humiliation and damage to self-esteem that can occur as the result of such an action (or even the threat of such an action) are sometimes irreparable. Many parents report incidents like this that occurred to them 30 or more years before, but which still raise the same devastated feelings. The outcome may not simply be avoidance of written work, but may well develop into a significant phobia related to a wide range of academic tasks, and even to school attendance, that sometimes even presents as a form of post-traumatic stress disorder, with its flashbacks, nightmares, and other significant psychological symptoms.

Set up for success

Please think very carefully before depriving a child of recess, particularly those whose gross motor skills are good and who have good energy levels. The frustration of struggling with printing or writing hour after hour can cause incredible fatigue for children with genuine difficulties, and they need a change of scenery, pace, and activity. It is important to set a number of small goals that can be accomplished and to reinforce positively the small steps. Children seldom object to recording their own successes in a small notebook dedicated to this purpose and this type of "success" book rarely gets lost en route to home. However, it is essential to be alert for children who procrastinate with work in the classroom so that they have to take it home to do, especially if this work comes back completed perfectly when you do not see evidence of the same quality in class. If you know they *can* work faster and better, some incentives to do so can be effective.

Reducing drills

If it is clear that the child understands the general concept being taught, you might consider reducing the quantity of output required on routine drills by having them complete every second question, for example. However, this only applies in situations where the written word is secondary to the concept being learned, and does not mean that a child with visual-motor difficulties should not be expected to practice basic skills. This requires some sensitivity to the child's difficulties and needs, and is a judgement call. Parents and teachers need to cooperate and collaborate on setting expectations in this area, rather than being on opposite sides.

Personal best

Setting individual goals by having the child compete against his or her previous performance is a way to motivate without comparing the child to the extremely competent children in the class; for example, asking for "one more than yesterday" or seeing "if you can beat your best time." Children sometimes prefer to time themselves, if they are able to do so, and often like to keep "records." Be very cautious about public displays of progress. This does not mean abandoning reinforcement/incentive systems, nor does it mean giving every child in the class a first prize. It simply means that a system whereby each child can be rewarded for personal improvement can work to motivate and reinforce effort and small successes.

Reading comprehension issues

It is necessary to be alert to the fact that many tests that purport to measure such abilities as reading comprehension actually measure children's ability to *write* and not their comprehension at all. It may be necessary to check out their actual understanding orally. It is especially important to ensure that quiet or introverted children are neither overlooked, nor singled out to perform in front of the whole group if no one else has to do this.

Flexible timelines and extended time

It is almost always necessary to offer flexible time to children whose writing is slow. However, most children, some bright children in particular, are sensitive to being constantly last to finish. It is therefore useful to start slower children ahead of time, or allow them to start or continue a written assignment at times when they have completed other work quickly and have some down time. Programs such as Precision Writing can help to speed up the slow writer, but require patience. *Please do not forget that giving a child extra time to finish a set amount of work does not help to increase the child's speed.* While it is probably the most common of all suggestions made for children with written expressive difficulties, allowing extra time does not increase speed of production – in fact, quite often the reverse. If improved speed of written output is the goal, then there are two ways to accomplish this: (a) to hold the amount of material constant and expect it to be completed in progressively shorter time periods; and (b) to hold the time period constant and to expect more work done in that set amount of time. Practice is the only way to accomplish this. Extra time can, of course, be given as a means to ensure that a particular task is completed. Individuals with nonverbal learning disabilities (NLD) often need specific coaching as to how to use that extra time effectively.

Learning ahead

For children with spelling difficulties, providing a list of "jargon" words in a particular subject area ahead of time can allow them to familiarize themselves prior to the unit being taught. This is a way of preventing the cumulative lag that develops when they get behind in their written work.

Printing versus cursive writing

Waiting for a child to perfect printing skills prior to starting cursive writing instruction is usually a waste of time. They may never print perfectly, and can benefit from learning the cursive formations along with everyone else. Some children, however, have never really been *taught* to print. They have been expected to pick it up by osmosis. Thus, in the early grades, it is often worth some re-teaching, which is best done in small group settings. If they have difficulty learning the cursive script, they may constantly switch to printing. If it is not specifically a cursive writing exercise, it really helps if you can be flexible. They often also have difficulty using a pen, so it often helps if you can be flexible in allowing the use of pencils. Left-handed children, in particular, often smudge their work when using a pen or a marker, which adds to their difficulties. There are, however, many adults who print rather than write. As long as the output is legible and can be performed quickly, who cares?

Calligraphy

Surprisingly, children who have difficulty with their handwriting often enjoy calligraphy, especially those who are extremely creatively artistic. This can be incorporated as part of their daily work, or can be given as an extra project for spare moments.

Keyboarding

Teaching computer keyboarding skills is usually extremely useful. It should be remembered, however, that fine motor difficulties can make the coordinated movements needed to touch-type quite a problem, so these children need patience and flexibility in learning the keyboard. Allowing them to play games at the computer that require knowledge of where the letters are can often lead to incidental learning and can be fun. There are a number of interesting and engaging software programs that systematically teach appropriate fingering and eventually bilateral touch-typing skills. However, indiscriminate and unsupervised use of the computer using a joystick or a mouse does not accomplish this learning goal – nor many others, in fact. While many people encourage it, we are a long way from each child in every classroom having access to an individual computer. In addition, children will be children, and laptops are lost or abused. The use of an AlphaSmart™, which is a word-processing-only device, can often be useful in a classroom setting, with the ability to download the content onto a regular computer at a later time.

Dictating

Many parents act as secretaries for their children, and as such chain themselves in to the process, often having trouble extricating themselves from this role. Teaching children how to dictate on to a tape recorder can be beneficial. They need to be taught step by step: turning the machine on, inserting the tape correctly, familiarity with all the controls (starting, stopping, rewinding, pausing, etc.), getting used to listening to their own voice. Then it is important to teach them how to listen to what they have dictated and gradually to transcribe using the pause button to give them time to write. It is useful to start with a simple spelling list or a French dictation, and gradually progress to phrases, sentences, and eventually paragraphs and/or stories.

Teaching editing skills

Teaching all children to edit their own work is useful and eventually time-efficient. Simply having them read aloud what they have written is a good first step and results in the correction of careless errors. (Sometimes you will be surprised that one or two children cannot read back what they have written only seconds or minutes before. This is a whole different ball-game and indicates a different set of difficulties.) Going through the work with them and underlining what needs to be corrected, then helping them to correct it (by re-teaching if necessary), is the next step. Following this, you can underline and encourage them to make the corrections; and finally, the child can be encouraged to find his or her own errors and correct them independently.

Editorial assistance

If a child uses a word processor with a spell-check program, or has a parent or "study buddy" to whom he or she dictates, teachers often feel that this is "cheating," when in fact it can be a useful step in the process of encouraging improvement. If you suspect that the parent or buddy is doing a lot more than simply transcribing what is said, have the child write his or her rough copy with no regard for editing or spelling, and then hand it in, along with the edited copy. If children cannot type, they often appreciate a story that they have written being typed up for them. Parent volunteers or students on work placements can often undertake this task in collaboration with the teacher.

Scribing

For individuals with significant written expressive difficulties, the request is often made for them to have an official "scribe," someone who does the writing work for them. Before such a major and expensive accommodation is put in place, it is critical to ensure that the child him or herself is putting in maximum effort.

Providing a "servant" for a child who then abdicates any and all responsibility for written work is reinforcing the wrong message. Good writing behavior includes sitting up straight, holding the pen or pencil properly, attending to what needs to be done, practicing basic skills even when we don't want to, supporting the paper with our other hand, accepting responsibility, and generally making an effort. A scribe is no substitute for hard work and practice. At the very least, the NLD individual should learn to dictate into a tape recorder or onto the computer, so that there is an oral record of the original work. As parents, we know how totally impossible it is to transcribe a child's verbal effort without some level of editing!

Spelling

There is little more discouraging and depressing to a child than to get back a piece of work covered in red ink, negative comments, and corrections. They often glance at it and become too anxious to be able to learn anything from it. The following may help:

- underlining two or three key words that are misspelled and encouraging the child to self-correct

- keeping a personal spelling book of new words, or words that the child commonly misspells, so that they can look them up themselves, recognizing that people who cannot spell also often have difficulty using dictionaries

- deducting a maximum number of marks for spelling (say, 5%) on any assignment for which spelling is *not* the main purpose

- recognizing that spelling can be taught and that most poor spellers can improve, although they may never be perfect

- realizing that it is your responsibility to *teach* spelling, and that most of these children do not learn simply by being exposed, say through a Whole Language approach

- understanding that they do not make these errors on purpose and that they are usually extremely upset by them; in fact, many are perfectionists and suffer high levels of anxiety over their written work

- utilizing the resource teacher, if available, to implement a spelling program, recognizing that there are a number of computer programs that can help

- having the child copy two or three key words two or three times, so that the correct form stands some chance of being recognized and remembered

- never expecting a child to write out a word more than three times, or the exercise completely loses its purpose; instead, encourage the child to write it once correctly, cover it up, and see if he or she can write it without looking, and then once or twice more as an insurance

- do not permit any child to exhibit publicly any work that contains uncorrected spelling errors, unless you are *absolutely* sure that you have important reasons for doing so; humiliating or punishing a child, or holding him up as an example of how things should not be done, are *not* good enough reasons.

Positive practice

The fine motor system and the visual system are closely located in the brain, as well as having many associations and interconnections between them. There is much evidence to support the interrelated nature of these two systems, and the fact that writing out a word will provide important motor feedback, allowing the pattern of the word to be encoded through a different pathway. This enhances memory for that word, not simply improving the chances of remembering it the next time we are called upon to write it, but also improving the chances of reading that word correctly. This means that it is important to make sure that the final pattern encoded by the fine motor system is the correct one. This means writing the whole word two or three times from beginning to end, without correction, so that it is more likely to be stored as one unit.

Speech/voice recognition software

Speech recognition software is another tool of the millennium. There are some relatively cheap programs that can translate the spoken word directly into the written word. While they used to be out of reach of many families because of the sophistication of equipment required, technological advances have provided increased accessibility. Most recently, the advent of software geared for children (e.g. SpeakQ – see: www.wordq.com) has opened up more possibilities. However, a big investment of time is required, along with endless patience, in order to train the computer to recognize one's voice, vocabulary, and phrasing. It can be overwhelming, even for most adults with no learning difficulties, to master the techniques that will result in efficient use of this tool. Good visual recognition skills are essential, plus adequate or better reasoning abilities, in order to make the corrections necessary to result in a good finished product. Nonetheless, there is no question that its use marks a significant step forward in compensatory strategies for individuals with visual-motor and/or fine motor problems.

Alternative means of evaluation

In order to evaluate what a child has learned, teachers may consider very carefully whether it is vital for the child to write the information or whether an alternative means of evaluation and assessment could be used. Having the child write what he can, and then going over it with him in a warm and friendly atmosphere, can sometimes provide important insights into what he has actually learned. Allowing point-form answers or (if possible) multiple-choice formats can help, although if the child has a visual-perceptual problem underlying the written expressive difficulty, he often becomes confused with computer-ready answer sheets and strict time limits. However, it needs to be recognized that not all evaluation methods lend themselves to equivalent alternatives, and students can be coached in different ways of studying for different types of tests or exams.

Alternative means of expression

In an effort to help children with written expressive difficulties, teachers frequently assign project work that involves building models, creating dioramas, making papier-mâché representations, and so on. Although many of them express themselves well through artistic media, it should be remembered that NLD children may also have difficulties with this type of project because of problems with space, perspective, and so on. Giving them more appropriate jobs to do or roles to play in group work, such as being the ideas person, or providing the verbal script might be more suited to their talents and strengths, and may be a better way to evaluate what they know.

"Special twice"

It is especially important for an intellectually superior or gifted youngster to receive special attention in his or her areas of strength that does not involve written work. Allowing oral presentations, construction projects, drama, musical, or artistic productions, and other alternative means of expression can often open up a shut-down child and encourage creativity. The earlier story about the profoundly gifted boy who was already showing high levels of frustration in Grade 1 is an illustration of how one's gifts and talents need to be recognized, but that they sometimes lead to high expectations and even higher levels of stress. Some empathy is important in order to support these children with two exceptionalities both to develop their talents, and to find ways to remediate their difficulties without sacrificing one for the other.

Developmental Coordination Disorder – strategies for success

CONTRIBUTED BY CHERYL MISSIUNA, PH.D. AND O.T. REG. (ONT.) OCCUPATIONAL THERAPIST, SCHOOL OF REHABILITATION SCIENCE, MCMASTER UNIVERSITY, HAMILTON, ONTARIO, AND HEAD OF CANCHILD, AND DENISE DELAAT, OCCUPATIONAL THERAPIST, CHILDREN'S HOSPITAL OF EASTERN ONTARIO

Children with DCD experience significant difficulty with everyday tasks. Their treatment and management is a source of great debate because little is understood about the cause of the disorder. Various treatments have been influenced by competing theories on motor development and motor skill acquisition.

Treatment approaches in DCD can be divided into two broad theoretical perspectives. The more traditional or "bottom-up" approaches seek to improve motor performance by attempting to remediate the central nervous system (sensory integration therapy, process-oriented therapy, perceptual-motor therapy). In contrast, contemporary or "top-down" approaches (task specific intervention, cognitive approaches) focus on affected functional activities in the context of the child's environment (Mandich *et al.* 2001). A review of the treatment literature over the past 15 years indicates that there is limited evidence to support the assumed relationship between underlying processes and functional performance (Pollock 2006; Wilson 2005). Top-down approaches, on the other hand, are showing some effectiveness in improving function in activities of daily living (Missiuna, Rivard and Pollock 2004; Polatajko *et al.* 2001) and the ability to generate effective strategies to solve their own movement problems (Sangster *et al.* 2005).

Families, parents, teachers, and other professionals often ask what they can do now to assist a child who is struggling with a coordination issue. The MATCH strategy described by Missiuna, Rivard and Pollock (2004) is a simple and effective method that ensures that the motor task and the learning environment are adjusted to enhance the performance of the child. Teachers and parents think about tasks that are difficult for the child and then try to:

- Modify the task
- Alter your expectations
- Teach strategies
- Change the environment
- Help by understanding.

The *CanChild* website (www.canchild.ca) has flyers for teachers that are specific to each grade level. Each flyer identifies school-related tasks that are difficult for children with DCD and then suggests specific ways to MATCH the task to the child's abilities. This website also has information for parents, health professionals, and members of the community.

And finally...good manners!

If we are privileged to have the support of a scribe, a study buddy whose notes we utilize, teachers who put themselves out to provide services above and beyond the call of duty, and/or parents who invest time and effort, it is imperative that we teach children to value this support, and to behave accordingly. A word of thanks, a gesture of appreciation, a short note, a positive phone call, a random act of kindness – all are necessary, both on the part of the children and their significant others. For children with NLD, this also provides a small but significant opportunity to develop a sense of empathy.

Just a reminder that a positive attitude, some common-sense, flexibility and patience are the most valuable assets when helping individuals with written expressive difficulties.

Chapter 15

STRATEGIES FOR MATHEMATICS

There are few academic areas that require a wider range of cognitive ability and problem-solving skills than mathematics, which is why it is simplistic to label someone as having a "mathematics disorder" or an "arithmetic or mathematical subtype," since this tells us nothing about the specific nature or source of the difficulties. Individuals with language-based problems have difficulties with math because of the need to learn a specific vocabulary and language that signal the various operations that have to be applied. Some individuals manage just fine in math until they are required to read the questions in written form. Memory difficulties of any kind will disrupt the wide range of information processing channels, both verbal and nonverbal. Problems with executive functions, such as planning, organizing, monitoring, and checking, will impede the logical thinking required to work through a series of operations to reach one, and only one, correct solution. Even if there are no barriers to numerical reasoning, there may well be difficulties in the translation of the thinking process onto paper, with the strict conventions of written mathematics and its symbolic formulations, from simple numerals to complex equations, graphs, and functions, to fractals, and advanced engineering applications.

Identification of the problem

The initial requirement when attempting to remediate problems with math is to determine precisely how far back we need to go in order to reach a solid foundation. For many individuals, this means extremely basic numeracy skills: counting one-to-one; matching quantities; understanding simple concepts of quantity such as same/different, more/less, bigger/smaller, add to/take from, once/twice/ten times, half/double, and so on. This investigation is easy to do when a child is young and in the first couple of grades of school, because this knowledge forms a major part of the math curriculum, and teaching these concepts is natural and anticipated for teachers. Once this train has left the station, however, and a child finds himself left behind, there is often great resistance on the part of teachers, parents and the child himself to revisit what is seen as "babyish" and what often creates some social difficulties with peers. However, pinpointing the areas of weakness in the basic foundations is essential if the rest of the mathematics structure is to be built.

De-cluttering

Because children with nonverbal learning disabilities (NLD) have problems with visual overload, it is important that all extraneous visual input be removed from their math work. This means, for example, providing them with worksheets that have only a few math examples per page – for some children, even one example at a time. If the math text is particularly decorative and distracting, this is likely to bother more children than those with NLD or Attention Deficit Hyperactivity Disorder (AD/HD), and teachers may need to be alert to this problem. Individuals with NLD need to be taught to do their own de-cluttering, by using plain paper to cover other examples while they are working, and by ensuring that their working area is as free as possible from visual distractions. These children probably work better at individual desks, rather than at a work table with other children – but then so do most children.

Teaching basic numeracy

As mentioned elsewhere in this guide, we should never forget that we are not all born with the basic skills required for learning, and we should therefore be aware that, although some children acquire basic numeracy simply from living life, others do need to be specifically taught. This is the case, regardless of what the most recent curriculum document says, or what the latest bandwagon is. Using fingers at the same time as counting out loud will help the NLD child to associate auditory, visual, and motor patterns, and increase the chances of learning. Children should never be told not to use their fingers for this very reason. Manipulatives, such as different colored or different length rods, or blocks, or coins, or beads – whatever – need to be on hand, and *associated* simultaneously with the appropriate words. The visual symbol associated with the number also needs to be integrated into the learning, so that the visual array representing actual quantity (e.g. 12 buttons) can be associated with the word (i.e., "twelve" or "a dozen") and with the written symbol 12, all at the same time. The child needs to be able to switch from one to the other, back and forth, until this skill becomes automatic.

Counting on

The ability to hold a number in our heads and count on from that number is vital in enabling us to calculate using numbers greater than ten. Most children are thrilled at being able to start at "ten thousand" and count to "ten thousand and five" – and enjoy this more than, say, "twelve plus five." Again, it is critical to associate the verbal/auditory/visual and linguistic elements of this skill by including pictures, objects, fingers, whatever, so that the patterns are established in more than one modality.

Visualization

The ability truly to understand the relationships involved in quantity, time, distance, and speed require us to use our visual imagination in order to create pictures – of elephants, of pies or pizzas, of boxes and fields and cylinders and the movement of a train that leaves New York at midnight, traveling at a given speed. That children all have this ability is often assumed, and much of math teaching is based on this assumption. However, many individuals with NLD have great difficulty creating pictures in their mind's eye, let alone manipulating that picture to add more, take some away, calculate trajectories, and so forth. It is therefore necessary when helping individuals with NLD with math, however basic, to ensure that these visual images are available. A quick test is to ask someone to visualize a tree and to describe it to you. If there is no ability to create the picture out of nothing, then pictures need to be provided. This does not mean that math books need to be full of pictures. Absolutely not. In fact, the visual image provided to a child in order to help him or her hook up the visual pattern with the appropriate auditory and verbal patterns needs to be as simple and unadorned as possible, containing only the relevant information. There may need to be multiple exposures to this image, along with the other sensory associations, before it is firmly entrenched. Thus, practice, practice, practice is the order of the day. If this type of visualization experience can be extended to home as well as school, so much the better. The number of forks required for dinner can be calculated by visualizing the members of the family who will be eating. Packing a bag for a trip can involve helping a child to visualize what he will be doing when he gets there, what he can "see" himself needing, and how many sets of underwear will be needed if he changes it once a day for a week.

Visualization of sets

Vital in the use of the basic operations (addition, subtraction, multiplication, and division) is the ability to look at quantity and change it in some way. Quite apart from learning the rules of operations and the rote learning of number facts, which can go a long way, the true understanding of relationships among numbers is facilitated by being able to "see" them as sets. We can then add to them, take from them, or divide and recombine them. We can subdivide them in to equal sets ($12 = 3 \times 4$ or 4×3, or 2×6 or 6×2) or unequal sets (12 + one set of ten and two sets of one). The understanding of sets is critical if we are to progress to the more complex concepts such as factoring, fractions, decimals, ratios, and beyond. Again, it is important to be aware that this skill can be taught, and that it needs to bridge the various pattern modalities (visual, auditory, language, motor).

Self-talk

The major way in which visual information is translated into other modalities, especially language and auditory, is for us to talk to ourselves as we think and work. In the area of math, this means reading the question aloud before we start the calculation – not simply the words of the question, but the number sentence itself. In this way, we are far less likely to make $19 + 8 = 9$, or $47 - 31 = 78$. It also means talking through each step of a more complex problem out loud, not only so that we can feed the information in through a different route, but also, and sometimes more importantly, so that people who are trying to help us can actually listen to our logic and our problem-solving attempts. It also allows us to pick up small mistakes because we realize that we have just heard ourselves say something that doesn't make sense. As mentioned elsewhere, the best way to teach self-talk is to model and demonstrate it, not simply to demand it.

Rote learning

A little while ago, I was speaking to hundreds of elementary teachers at a workshop on NLD, and asked them how many of them had their students "chant" their multiplication tables. To my surprise and consternation, only about three hands were raised. There is little point in trying to find creative and unique strategies for remediating math problems if a whole approach to learning is ignored because it is considered to be obsolete, or old-fashioned. "We just don't do it that way any more," I was told by one teacher afterwards, while another told me that she was considered to be the school's Dragon Lady and Dinosaur by both her colleagues and parents alike, because she drilled math facts on a regular basis. There is absolutely no question that auditory patterning is critical in the learning of math facts – whether it is by repeating, by chanting, or by singing. At the risk of flogging a very dead horse, it is worth repeating that the auditory input created by repetition, chanting or singing needs to be paired with visual input wherever possible, and even if at all possible by using gross and fine motor skills at the same time. Numbers have a rhythm, and often rhyme, of their own, and can be clapped or danced. It is not until we recognize the patterns of number sequences that we can cope with numbers out of sequence. Therefore, flash cards only have utility once the basic patterns have been learned. Otherwise, a child is trying to remember a complex mosaic of, to him or her, isolated facts.

Rules

It is obvious to most of us that there are multiple rules associated with math. Along with the fact that there is a specific answer so we can satisfy our need for closure, that's what attracts those of us who are intrinsically enamored of order. To the math aficionado, there is beauty in the regularity and patterns that can be described by functions and other rules. If you want the answer to come out right, do it this way… Teachers and others do spend time putting operations into words (for example, "If the number is ten or more, you have to put the units here in the right-hand column, and then carry the one over here"). Children with NLD require these rules to be written down, not simply spoken, and need them associated in real time with the visual example, and preferably with other pictures if at all possible. The use of color coding can be very beneficial. For example, the verbal rule can be highlighted in the same color as the stage of the operation in numerical form. In long division, this would translate to: divide (pink), multiply (yellow), subtract (blue), bring down (green).

Tricks and shortcuts

Quite apart from the standard rules of how to perform various mathematical operations, there are many little tricks or shortcuts that are known and used by many of us. It is important to share all of these with our NLD children, so that they can see that there are often neat ways that we can reach the same point on the learning map, and that it usually doesn't matter how we get there. Many of us do not know the rules about odd and even numbers: for example, adding, multiplying, or dividing two even numbers will always result in an even number; multiplying odd numbers will always result in an odd number; subtracting an odd number from an even number will result in an odd number. Accompanied by visual illustrations or actual manipulatives, these rules will be seen, rather than simply heard. Teach children tricks such as how to do the nine-times-table using their fingers: place hands palms up; number fingers from left to right from one through to ten; decide how many nines you need (e.g. six times nine); put that finger down into the palm. The number of fingers to the left of the target finger will be the number of tens (in the case of six times nine this will be five fingers, or 50); the number of fingers to the right of the target finger will be the number of units (in this case, four). Thus the answer is 54. Teaching a trick such as this has as a bonus the sense of pride the child feels in mastering something that perhaps no one else in the family knows. There may well be self-help books out there that demonstrate tricks and shortcuts such as this, so search around, and survey friends, relatives, and anyone else you can think of to find out what they know. Whatever we may be told, there is no substitute for finding ways to learn something that stick in our mind.

Home-baked math

Unlike the teenager who confided that he had no need to learn math, because there was no math in his life, most of us realize that our lives are filled with numbers and math concepts. We shop, we cook, we earn, we pay, we make change, we balance cheque books, we travel distances at varying speed, we calculate how much meat to buy for a dinner party of eight, we learn routines for dance recitals, we get out of the way of a speeding car, we know when a bag is too heavy, and we know that we need to get from here to there. For many children, the symbols they learn in the classroom are easily translated into real life. For children with NLD, this is not usually the case. Therefore, it is vital to integrate their school-based math learning into daily life as immediately and as thoroughly as possible, again so that the

ve received can be translated into real experi-
:lp with math, there is no better way to do this
" experiences and to use them as a teaching

e Golick 1988), there are many board games and
ers. Games that involve matching (e.g. Snap, Go
ng quantity (e.g. War), which in turn are easier
y of thinking and higher level calculations (e.g.
Rummy, Canasta, Cribbage). However, many NLD children enjoy playing cards, and all games will provide some experience with numbers and associated concepts. Given that your NLD child or student will be outclassed perhaps even by much younger siblings, it is important to ensure that turn-taking is firmly enforced, and/or that the level of the questions is appropriate for the child.

Second language learning and math

Before reaching the age for formal math learning, children have had a wealth of experiences that they bring to the learning situation. All of these experiences are encoded in verbal memory in their mother tongue. During World War II, it was common to ask captives or potential spies to count quickly from one to ten in order to determine true nationality, because this ability is so entrenched within our language of thought that it becomes truly automatic. When we teach children numeracy skills in a second language, after their mother tongue is well established, it is important to recognize that they may not immediately connect this new information with their existing knowledge. They may learn the rules in the second language, and certainly will know the vocabulary of operations in the second language, without ever making the very necessary connections with real-life math situations. The silver lining is that they do specifically learn the appropriate jargon, and can also learn the rules verbally.

Teacher and parent variables

It is often the case that teachers who choose to teach French in a French Immersion setting are not, by calling, mathematicians – which can actually be said for many kindergarten or elementary grade teachers, regardless of language of instruction. This can cause some difficulty when they are required to teach "outside the box," so to speak, in terms of trying different ways of teaching the same patterns, concepts, or skills. Many teachers can only teach math the way the textbook tells them to, and are nervous, or sometimes even hostile, about alternative methods that succeed in getting the information in and understood. On the other hand, it is frequently quite difficult for someone for whom math comes easily, and for whom the patterns and processes are patently obvious, to teach someone who does not see the world the same way, especially if that individual becomes quickly exasperated with the child's lack of pattern recognition skills. In general, if a child is having difficulty, at least in the younger grades, it is often better for the parent who is least comfortable with math to work through the examples with the child – thinking aloud, thinking together, and trying to figure it out collaboratively.

Calculators, computers, and accountants

It is always a judgement call when to allow children to use calculators or other tools to help them with math. A general rule of thumb is that calculators don't help you to extract the correct number sentence or what mathematical operations to use, so in terms of the goals of the particular learning module, they may not be relevant.

If an individual has managed to work through the problem to the point where he or she can tell you what operations are needed and what numbers are to be plugged in, there may be some merit in utilizing a calculator to check an answer. However, when the goal is to practice number facts to the point where they become automatically accessible, it is clear that calculators should not be used. Computer software that teaches number facts through "games" can be very useful, especially if there is a difficulty component built in that challenges a child to rise to different levels. Computers allow children to make their mistakes privately. The advantage of this is avoidance of the humiliation that comes from working at a level way below your classmates. The caution is that the child needs to be monitored, because a computer doesn't care if you get the response by trial and error.

Gender issues

Although I fervently wish it were not the case, we occasionally encounter the age-old bias that girls simply are not meant to be competent in math. Nothing could be further from the truth, but the myth persists. Sometimes, unfortunately, it is we females who are our own worst enemy. As one mother told me, when asked if there were any messages being given to her daughter at home about math competence: "Well, if there are, they would come from her father, because I don't do math." While every cell in the female brain contains a different mix of hormones and chromosomes from male brain cells, and while there is research to support differences in a number of anatomical structures between the sexes, there is absolutely no evidence to support basically differential ability levels. There has been much support for many years for the notion of single-gender classrooms for both math and science, since it has been shown that girls do much better in this environment than they do in a co-educational setting. With our NLD children, we must ensure that there are no sociological issues compounding what is already a sensitive issue.

Chapter 16

STRATEGIES FOR SELF-REGULATION

In order to address some of the attentional fluctuations that frequently accompany nonverbal learning disabilities (NLD), in addition to many of the suggestions in the previous few sections, the following may be helpful. While they are primarily geared to classroom and other group activities, most of them are also relevant at home, particularly during family times, such as meals, outings, and so on.

Getting a child's attention

It helps to use a child's name when addressing her; touching her shoulder if necessary to get her attention. Getting down to a child's level and speaking in a low voice can often be more effective than raising one's voice.

Teaching waiting and listening behaviors

Although it would be useful if they were, waiting and listening behaviors are not innate. They are social behaviors that need to be taught. If children have every whim instantly gratified, and are never expected to wait for anything, they may never learn how. "Good waiting" and "good listening" need to be specifically defined. Waiting behavior often involves silence! Thus, paying attention to a child every time that child interrupts, whines, or badgers in fact reinforces all of those negative behaviors. If we respond each time, we are, in fact, modeling the exact opposite of the waiting behaviors we are trying to teach our children. Good listening usually involves being still, looking at the person who is speaking, being silent, making an effort to understand and remember what is being said, and often checking out whether one has heard correctly. Active listening also involves asking questions and seeking clarification. Children need to learn that waiting often pays off, so if we have told a child to wait, and then forget to get back to them, we may not be helping to teach that very important lesson.

Self-soothing

Rather than depending upon external sources for comfort, we pretty soon have to learn that there are times when we need to comfort ourselves. Some infants self-soothe by thumb-sucking or holding on to a blanket or soft toy. Older children choose sleep toys, favorite books or activities, movies, or video games. Teens may choose TV or music. Some rely on substances, so not all self-soothing behaviors are necessarily those we would choose for our children. However, if we are to regulate our own behavior, it is necessary to look at ways we can do this without relying on others to do it for us. Again, if we, as parents, are always at a child's beck and call, that child may miss out on learning that he or she is, in fact, in possession of ways in which to provide comfort, or at least to tide him or herself over until someone else is available. Introverted children are far more competent at self-soothing than are extroverted children who need people around in order to reduce anxiety.

Preferential seating

In order to eliminate unnecessary stimulation in the classroom, it helps to place a child as close to the teacher as possible during structured group activities and perhaps next to a child who can provide a good model. It is often recommended that a child with attentional difficulties be placed in a highly structured classroom. This is obviously important for the monitoring and clear guidelines that these children need. It has to be borne in mind, however, that their attentional difficulties will, in fact, be much more obvious in such a setting, rather than in a free-flow, high activity level classroom. This is not the child's fault.

Activity breaks

It is impossible for most of us to concentrate for long periods of time, and most of us need breaks. Children who have difficulty with self-regulation will need to be encouraged to find a rhythm or pattern of energy that works best for them. Some can be encouraged to focus for 15 or 20 minutes, followed by a similar period of activity, after which they can get back to settling down again. Others may be difficult to settle after a break period, and may work better for a slightly longer period, knowing that they will then be free. It is important for parents to encourage times at home when there is little activity required (down times) as well as periods when children are required to be more active. These times need to be labeled clearly as "down time" or "activity time" which will allow the child with NLD to associate the particular activity level with a set of verbal expectations. Similarly, it is necessary to impose definite boundaries between work time and play time, since it is often hard for the NLD child to moderate his or her behavior appropriately for the expectations of the circumstances.

Self-talk

Encouraging the child to use self-talk when she plays or works helps her to slow down and to keep herself on task. This means that the adult needs to model self-talk, and that the child needs to be able to talk aloud without being reprimanded for disturbing others. Teaching a child to whisper, to talk under her breath, and eventually to talk silently inside her head, will be necessary. This includes reading written instructions and math questions (even simply saying the numbers and the operation required) out loud so that the child's stronger auditory and verbal systems will be engaged.

Stop–look–listen

In an effort to encourage children to control their impulses, it can be helpful to employ some verbal/visual strategies. Because the color red is associated with stop, and green with go, a paper disc with red on one side and green on the other can be placed on the child's desk, or in front of his plate at a mealtime. He can then be taught that when the red side is exposed, he is not supposed to be engaging in any activity other than listening or looking. As soon as the disc is turned over to the green side, he can begin or continue whatever activity is required. Using a traffic light approach, and including a yellow signal, we can teach children to engage in planning what they are going to do. When they tell us what that is, to our satisfaction, the "light" changes to green, and they are permitted to go ahead. The advantage of this system for NLD children is that they can learn to associate a visual stimulus (i.e. color) with verbal information and action, thus effecting the cross-modal pattern transfer.

Lists

Give the child a simple list (made up of drawings or pictures for younger children) of small steps when she is expected to follow a routine alone, so that she can refer to it and check off what she has completed. This may be useful for some home routines (bedtime, getting ready to leave in the morning, tidying up, etc.) as well as for daycare or school. The more she is involved in composing the list, the more likely she is to use it. She will need help at first learning how to work through each step, and consistent monitoring until each step becomes automatic. A list that consists of "I" statements in the past tense (e.g. "I wrote out my spelling words three times" or "I put all my books back on the shelf") assists a child to own her own behavior, to see that it is anticipated that the task will be completed, and encourages independence from adults. ("Come back and see me when your list is done.") For some children, it is useful to incorporate a statement such as: "Even though I think it is stupid, I made my bed" or "Even though I wanted to watch TV, I got on with my homework right after supper." This allows children to learn that we sometimes have to do things even when we don't feel like doing them. While it is overwhelming to have too many lists at any one time, in general whenever there is a routine to be followed that consists of discrete steps, it is worth a try, especially if we find ourselves saying the same things over and over again.

Positive reinforcement

It is very important to ensure that you praise a child's efforts and small steps toward success. This does not have to be elaborate or overdone – just a simple acknowledgement ("Good work," "Nice listening," "Thanks for doing that," etc.). Saying something like "It's about time!" does not count as reinforcement.

Focusing to learn

The following suggestions are taken from *TRICS for Written Communication* by Susan J. Amundson (1998). While intended primarily for the classroom, these suggestions are worthwhile for other situations requiring concentration and focus, especially during study times.

- *Monitor the room temperature.* Cool, fresh air helps students attend more than warm, stale air. Adjust the classroom temperature accordingly.

- *Use predictable, firm touch.* When touching or hugging a child who is sensitive to touch, use deep, firm pressure. Light touch may be aversive.

- *Moderate voice and verbal directions.* Simplifying verbal instructions and keeping the volume of voice down often helps students focus and follow directions.

- *Place inflatable seat cushions in student' chairs to improve focusing.* Squirmy or lethargic students may benefit from an inflatable seat cushion on the chair. Commercially available cushions are of soft plastic, available in wedge or disc shapes and child sizes, and are easily inflated like a balloon. An economical cushion is a partially inflated beach ball. The cushions may help squirmy students by providing more sensorimotor input so it is not sought out of their chairs. For lethargic students, inflatable cushions may arouse their sensorimotor systems and improve engagement in desktop activities. Students react individually to inflatable seat cushions and need to be well monitored.

- *Use non-skid material in student' chairs.* Some students slip out of plastic, molded chairs. Place a piece of non-skid material, such as Dycem™ or boating mesh, in the seat to help the student sit upright.

- *Allow students to complete written work while lying on the floor.* Place the student on the floor with the writing assignment on a clipboard. When students write while lying on their stomachs, it may benefit them physically. If a soft bolster or rolled-up towel or blanket is placed under the student's chest, the pressure on the chest may be calming and organizing for the student. Carefully monitor this position.

- *Provide firm grounding toys for students who distract easily.* Handling firm, spongy toys may be grounding for the student. These grounding toys may help the student focus on the teacher, attend to school work, and sit quietly at the desk. Balloons filled with flour, rice, cornstarch or beans are economical grounding toys. Artist's erasers can be a grounding device. A large, resistive, stretchable eraser moved in the hands during listening times can help students focus and attend. An artist's eraser leaves no erasure markings and takes little effort. Ask an occupational therapy practitioner for other grounding toy suggestions.

- *Use manipulative grounding toys for students.* Small, hand-sized toys with interchangeable, manipulative parts can provide grounding and help certain students attend and focus in the classroom. Gadgets that rotate, twist, coil, and bend may be allowed, but should not distract others in the classroom.

- *Encourage students to complete worksheets while standing.* Tape the student's worksheet at eye level on a vertical surface. When writing in a standing position, some students become more attentive and focused.

- *Band chair legs with tubing.* Students needing sensorimotor input for grounding in order to focus on learning may push their chairs back and rock on the back legs. To help students get this input while sitting, use rubber bands from the inner tubes or car tires or use Theratubing™, and loop them around the front chair legs or the front legs of the desk. Students can push their legs against the band, gaining more sensorimotor input and focus for learning. Attach bands to the side of the chair for stretching the arms.

- *Introduce simple yoga postures for transitions.* For flexibility, strengthening and centering, students enjoy simple yoga poses. They are quiet in the classroom and work well to make students alert and grounded, and to build strength and flexibility. Contact an occupational or physical therapist for age-appropriate suggestions.

- *Use transitional activities to encourage students to be centered.* Activities that provide students with "heavy work" (i.e. resistance) may be calming and focusing, just as adults may find pushing a lawnmower or scrubbing a floor centering.

- *Provide chewy and crunchy snacks.* Although food is not widely promoted during class time, certain snacks may help students be calm and focus on their school work. Consider the following chewy treats: fruit roll-ups; dried fruits (raisins, apple slices, banana chips); beef and fish jerky; sugarless gum; sugar-free candies; bagels; cheese chunks. Crunchy snacks are: raw vegetable sticks; apple slices; pretzels; popcorn; bread sticks; rice cakes.

- *Provide students with appropriate objects to mouth when they are working.* Some students will suck on their hair, chew on erasers, place their fingers in their mouths, and/or grind their teeth. Most students do this to help themselves calm and focus. Allow the student to chew on a necklace strung with flexible rubber tubing pieces or a piece of washcloth.

- *Allow students to drink from water bottles.* Sucking through a straw may be calming for some students. Allow the student to have a water bottle with a plastic straw at the desk. By substituting a "crazy" (longer, coiled and looping) straw, the student must suck harder to move the water, which can be more organizing to the sensorimotor system.

In addition, it has been found that replacing the traditional student chair with a large exercise ball has been a calming influence for many fidgety children.

A note about medication

If a medical approach to the attentional difficulties exhibited by some children with NLD is to be considered (for example, the use of Ritalin or related substances), it is important to be aware of the fact that the primary problems for these children are the difficulties with pattern recognition, memory, and reproduction that underlie the learning disability. However, appropriate and well-monitored use of medication can help some NLD children to focus their attention, control hyperkinesis and impulsivity to some degree, increase the chances of them finishing assignments in a shorter time, allow them to produce neater written work, and reduce off-task behavior. The use of medication will *not* address the underlying perceptual and/or organizational deficits. Learning disabilities are not eliminated by the use of medication, and the associated social/behavioral difficulties, while sometimes managed, are not routinely "cured." It is also critical to remember that there is sometimes a high level of resistance to the use of medication by parents and/or students, frequently for good reason, and that sometimes the use of medication is contraindicated because of body mass index, allergies, co-existing disorders such as Tourette's Syndrome, or other important conditions. It is therefore inappropriate for parents to be placed in a position where they feel coerced into agreeing to medicate a child in exchange for the cooperation of the school in programming for that child. It is completely unacceptable for physicians to prescribe medication for children without an appropriate diagnostic process in place. It is equally unacceptable for those of us who may know one of these physicians to suggest to parents that they consult this individual in an attempt to by-pass the appropriate diagnostic process.

It is critical for parents to ensure that they are fully informed about medication issues, and to consult a trusted pediatrician, family physician, neurologist, or psychiatrist. Without a full and relevant psychological or psychoeducational assessment, however, even these consultations may be lacking much vital information.

Additional resources

There are numerous excellent sources for assisting with management of attention deficit disorders, and this is not the place to attempt to summarize this huge body of literature. The Learning Disabilities Associations or CHADD (Children and Adults with Attention Deficit Disorders) are helpful resources, and are listed in local telephone directories. Two particularly enjoyable and practical books are: *Driven to Distraction* (Hallowell 1995), and *The Manipulative Child* (Swihart and Cotter 1998). Russell Barkley's revised *Taking Charge of AD/HD, Revised Edition: The Complete, Authoritative Guide for Parents* (2000) contains a wealth of information.

Chapter 17

STRATEGIES FOR
BEHAVIOR MANAGEMENT

In general, there is a need to use the same basic approaches to behavior management that work for all children: state what you want them to do in positive terms, instead of what you do not want them to do; make sure you are being concrete and clear; use words and concepts they understand; give them a clear set of choices, any of which you can live with; explain what the consequence of each choice is; if there is no choice, do not give one; follow through. Simple, *n'est-ce pas?*

Identifying the pattern

When we are trying to teach a particular behavior pattern, it is necessary first to determine what that pattern is. This may seem like a very obvious statement. It is not. As adults, we are far too complex or vague, and we try to teach children to "behave appropriately," "show respect," "act responsibly," and other noble yet esoteric expectations. Children with nonverbal learning disabilities (NLD), because of their superior verbal abilities, may well appear to know these expectations. They can repeat them; they can even define them sometimes. However, for the most part they do not apply them when they need to be applied.

Predictability

For children who have great difficulty recognizing and learning patterns, it is extremely important to provide them with patterns that are consistently the same. If we tell them that Action A will lead to Consequence A, and that does, in fact, prove to be true, we have begun the pattern. If next time, Action A is again followed by Consequence A, that pattern becomes a little more established, and it will not be long before the child can begin to predict what will happen, given

Action A. All too frequently, however, we adults interfere with the learning of this pattern. We do not provide Consequence A. We forget. We're busy. We lecture instead. Or we provide some other consequence instead. This is not only confusing for the NLD child, it is downright anxiety-provoking, since it adds to the unpredictability of the world at large, and makes it even more difficult to navigate.

Follow-through

The major difference between NLD children and others is that they frequently find it difficult or impossible to imagine what a consequence is going to be like by visualizing it, or creating a hypothetical situation in their heads. They are concrete thinkers, and learn best from actual experience. While we hope that we do not have to let them touch the hot stove to find out that our warnings were correct, there is certainly an element of that in managing their behavior. It is, therefore, even more critical with NLD children than with others that we follow through with action! Words alone will not provide the necessary experiences that shape their future choices. We have to let the picture match the words. Follow-through, or meaning what we say, is critical for all children in order to establish and build trust relationships. It is even more critical for the NLD child in terms of establishing predictable behavioral and social patterns.

Encouraging independence

A child with NLD frequently generates a great deal of support from adults around her, both at home and elsewhere, since the need for adult intervention in a multitude of situations is usually quite obvious. Thus, she may inadvertently but frequently become quite dependent on adults and somewhat passive in owning and/or solving her own problems. There is, therefore, a real need for her to see herself as a competent child – being put in charge of those tasks for which she already has the appropriate developmental skills (such as putting on her jacket to go outside), being coached in skills that are emerging (such as following directions, or interactive play), and being given some small responsibilities in areas in which she is competent but that others do mostly for her (e.g. helping with simple household chores). A common issue in teaching a child to be independent is that accomplishing this goal often deprives others of a job! A full-time parent may feel guilty for insisting that a child do something without help. An educational assistant, employed to assist a child with NLD, may be seen as doing nothing if the child is encouraged to work by himself. Independence is a two-way street, and both parties need to be working toward the same goal. A child who has been receiving huge amounts of attention and help for a difficulty or problem of some kind often feels abandoned when things improve and therefore there may be some secondary gain to be had from not improving. There are some individuals who hold on to symptoms because of the reinforcement they receive, including an extra share of parental attention, particularly in a family where there are other siblings.

Choices and consequences

It is always important to follow through with the consequences of choices that a child makes; therefore, it is important for adults to give her a limited selection of choices with simple, predictable consequences, from which she can choose (e.g. "Would you like juice or milk?" "Would you like to stay here quietly or go to your room?" "Hurry and get into your pyjamas, then there'll be time for your story before you go to sleep"). In this way, she will be able to trust her environment more and reduce her anxiety levels. It is also, therefore, important that the consequences of her choices are in fact available to her, and preferable that the consequence be positive. If you are unwilling or unable to follow through with the consequence, it is usually wiser not to give the choice. It is important to recognize the difference between a free choice and a limited choice. Giving a child a free choice (e.g. "What would you like to do for your birthday this year?") will often lead to an unacceptable option ("I'd like to have my whole grade over for a sleep-over"). This results in a set-up for conflict, unless it is clearly presented as the first step in a brain-storming exercise, where all suggestions are admitted prior to reducing the set to feasible and acceptable options only. The better option is to provide a set of choices, any one of which is acceptable. In this way, the child learns to make choices within a safe, adult-supervised context. As children grow into adolescents and young adults, they take over increasing responsibility for the consequences of their choices. Maturity, or the end of adolescence, can be said to occur when we finally take over all responsibility for the consequences of our actions. Even then, however, as parents, we never knowingly let our children put themselves in danger, if we can possibly avoid it!

Non-negotiables

It is always important to remember that, in some situations, the child in fact has no choice. Thus, asking a child: "Would you like to put your toys away now and come for supper?" may be offering a non-existent choice, since the child is free to say "No" to the question, and mean it. Stating what you want, rather than asking, at least keeps everyone honest. "It is supper time. Please put your toys away now." "We are going to Grandma's for the weekend." "It's time to do your homework." Every family has its own set of non-negotiables. Safety issues tend to be at the top of the list. It is necessary to develop a way of differentiating between issues that can be debated, and those that cannot, especially for verbally precocious and verbally competent children who will keep us in court arguing their position for weeks. When it is decided that an issue is neither debatable nor negotiable, it is necessary to stop debating it and to stop negotiating it. This means depriving the verbally persistent child of an audience. Staying there debating why an issue is not debatable is inappropriate and sends the wrong message. "That's not up for discussion" is sufficient, provided we follow through.

Importance of not over-verbalizing

As with most children, it will be helpful to the child with NLD if adults do not over-verbalize to her, even though her verbal skills may be quite strong. There is a danger of overestimating the child's ability to understand the substance, not just the words, of what is being said. Nonverbal interactions are therefore important to develop: raising an eyebrow, folding arms, making eye contact, changing tone of voice to be appropriate to the feeling being expressed, taking her hand and removing her from a situation, containing a tantrum by holding her gently but firmly, and so on, are all very important. If you cannot be totally nonverbal, try the one word command: "Bed!" "Toys!" "Snowsuit!" "Story!" "Cuddle!" "Now!", or counting to three. Talking to her in a gentle, soothing, warm voice will convey a sense of caring, and will help to calm and relax her when she is upset.

"Chains" of behaviors

Some situations require children to learn to follow a string of simple behaviors that make up a more complex behavior. For example, she is required to perform several distinct tasks in order to get herself ready to go outside, or to put away her clothes when she comes inside again. In order to establish new strings, it will be important to encourage her to practice following the whole string from beginning to end without interruption or intervention. Thus, if she gets distracted in the middle, it will be best to have her go back to the beginning and start the whole sequence over. This is called "positive practice" and helps the child's whole body learn the behavior. If a child is required, for example, to walk into the classroom and take a textbook off the shelf before sitting down, he needs to be sent out of the classroom to start the sequence over as many times as is necessary to have him perform all three actions without any kind of interruption. If an adult is always there to remind him, this feature will become "chained" in as part of the overall action, and it will be hard to extricate that adult.

Advanced warning

It will be helpful to the child if she can be warned in advance of pending changes in routine. For example: "We are going to ask you to tidy up in a minute so that we can start Circle Time," or "After I count to three, I'd like you to be sitting on your chair ready for snack." Getting her involved in predicting what will come next in a daily routine will maximize the chances of her compliance. "Jesse, what are we going to do after we have tidied up?"

Positive "job descriptions"

All children benefit from having a positive "job description" – in other words, from being told what is expected, rather than what is not. "Jon, please keep your hands to yourself" is preferable to "Jon, please stop bothering people." In this manner, the adults can focus on and look for desired behaviors, and children receive attention for what they are supposed to be doing.

Have to and want to

For most children, NLD children being no exception, life is divided into "have to" and "want to" activities. The simplest form of behavior management consists of helping a child distinguish between the two sets, and then ensuring that the "have to" activities are completed before the "want to"s begin. In this way, the child is responsible for his or her own consequences, and there is no need for punishment. "Can I go out now?" "Please may I use the phone?" "How come I can't watch TV?" can all be responded to with a simple "Have you done what you have to do yet? If not, hurry up and get on with it! I know you want to go out/use the phone/watch TV! You can do that as soon as you're done." This approach helps the child own his own behavior, and stop blaming others for getting in the way of what he wants to do.

Nonverbal parenting

In an effort to model nonverbal behaviors, it is important that we teach our children through nonverbal means wherever we can. This includes such parenting behaviors as using overt body language to indicate our mood (e.g. hands on hips, frown, head tilted to one side, arms wide open, hugs, etc.), at the same time attaching a verbal label in a "paired-associate learning" kind of way. Facial expressions that reflect feelings again should be used and labeled. Rather than prattling on with our children's eyes glazing over, we can perform simple activities that give a big message: the compost bucket on my son's bed ensured that he never again forgot to put it outside; an empty plate at supper signaled that the dogs needed to be fed; a lack of response to a lack of "please" spoke louder than a whole lecture full of words. Because NLD children are so good at engaging us verbally, it is hard to parent them nonverbally. However, they learn more from concrete consequences (or lack of them).

Additional resources

Further discussion of this type of approach to behavior management can be found in *Who's in Charge? A Guide to Family Management* (Mamen 1997), *Laughter, Love and Limits: Parenting for Life* (Mamen 1998), and *The Pampered Child Syndrome: How to Recognize It, How to Manage it and How to Avoid It* (Mamen 2006).

Chapter 18

A FINAL FEW WORDS

As mentioned at the outset, the diagnosis of a nonverbal learning disability (NLD) is often complex, overwhelming, and sometimes even discouraging. Although it is now a more familiar term in the worlds of psychology and education, there is still some resistance to its acceptance as a legitimate diagnosis with a need for understanding and appropriate intervention. Prior to the identification of a learning disability of any kind, language-based or nonverbal, a full developmental or psychological assessment is critical, so that all aspects of the child's development can be explored, and so that the specific pattern of psychological process deficits can be identified for purposes of interventions, accommodations, and modifications. It is also important for the individual to have a full medical examination, including vision and hearing checks, and to consider the possibility of allergies being related to the erratic and somewhat cyclical nature of any behavioral concerns. It is also necessary to consider that the learning, social, behavioral, and emotional problems may be due to other similar and often related disorders such as Asperger's Syndrome, Developmental Coordination Disorder, Sensory Integration Disorder, Tourette's Syndrome, or Mild Intellectual Delay. The picture is complicated by the fact that some of these disorders may co-exist.

Working or living with NLD can be strenuous and frequently frustrating, since the difficulties are often subtle and pervasive, and the rewards are long in coming. It is very important for parents and teachers of children with NLD, as well as individuals with NLD themselves, to find an individual or an organization, such as NLD Ontario or NLDline, who can provide information and support. Sometimes, one or both parents and/or teachers may themselves have some of the characteristics of NLD, and therefore require more specific assistance with parenting and teaching, since these are both jobs that utilize a great deal of nonverbal ability.

The need for parents, caregivers, extended family members, and teachers to work as a team cannot be stressed enough. It is important to establish a set of goals for each child that make sense in more than one context and that can be supported by all significant adults in the child's life, even though they may have different roles and different ways of journeying to the same destination. In terms of a broader support base, family physicians can be very helpful, as can public health nurses, special services personnel with daycare agencies and school boards, psychologists, occupational therapists, speech-language pathologists, physical therapists, social workers, special education specialists, family support workers, community resource centre staff, and others.

Whenever a child is having difficulties, it is extremely important for teachers and parents to liaise with each other to report positive progress, to set reasonable goals, to have an open agenda about what is or is not expected at home, and to confirm that it is the school system that has the responsibility for teaching the curriculum materials. It is not reasonable for schools to *expect* parents to teach academics. Some will, but the vast majority do not. Parents are responsible for valuing education in a general sense, being supportive, providing the opportunity for homework to be done, and reinforcing success. It is vitally important that a child who has difficulty completing independent written work *not* be sent home with the entire day's work to do with parents. This causes major problems in the majority of families, however nurturing and positive they are, and may be the source of incredible stress for the child. It is also vitally important that the parents know that the child is not completing work in the classroom and that something is being done at the school to rectify this situation.

There are many tutors and tutoring services in the community that parents will often use as a back-up or an alternative to whatever is (or is not) available through the school system. It is important to remember that whatever helps the child is the primary focus, regardless of who provides the support. Sometimes, it is difficult as a classroom teacher to be gracious about a subtle or not-so-subtle message that you are not doing your job properly, but parents often recognize (usually quite accurately) that teachers have neither the time nor the opportunity to teach each child one-on-one, and so they prefer to seek support elsewhere. While sometimes hard to do, it is important for teachers not to take this too personally and to try, if at all possible, to communicate with the tutor to ensure common goals. It does not, however, hurt for educators to take inventory and see whether they are missing the chance to help even in a small way. Most tutors are extremely eager and willing to liaise with both parents and teachers to ensure a united, predictable, and common front in order to reduce confusion and to simplify plans for the child.

Learning difficulties have been around for a long time and will continue to be ever present. The thrust in education is to integrate all kinds of children into the regular program, which frequently raises the anxiety levels of the regular class-room teacher. Do not forget to make use of the important network available to you from fellow staff and administrators. You will find many useful suggestions from your colleagues. There is no magic "fix" – just patience, understanding, persever-ance, and a flexible approach. A positive and optimistic attitude, along with a willingness to become involved, are the foundation upon which success is built – step by little step.

It is very important for teachers to remember that parents are usually trying to do a good job raising and educating their children. Feedback from teachers to parents of children with learning or behavioral difficulties tends to be overwhelm-ingly negative, to the point where a call from school can set up an almost phobic reaction in many mothers and fathers. A good rule of thumb is that it takes the same amount of time to make a positive, constructive phone call ("Just calling to tell you that Jason had a wonderful day") as it does to make a negative one ("Jason did not complete his work in class and had to miss recess again"), but the payoff is *considerably* greater. Bad news is received better if it is the filling in a positive sandwich. Parents sometimes need to be reminded of the same rule of thumb!

The triad of understanding–prediction–control is the foundation of good research. Once we understand a phenomenon, we can predict its occurrence, and hence, by manipulating certain variables, we can begin to control it. With NLD, we need to be able to recognize and identify patterns of strengths and weaknesses so that we can predict what is likely to happen, and hence initiate some interventions in order to manage the various difficulties that can otherwise occur. These are not only the goals for those of us who want to help, but are also ultimately the goals for individuals with NLD themselves.

Finally, it is vital to understand that NLD can indeed be understood, especially when broken down into manageable "chunks," and that they *can* be remediated. This can result in a renewed sense of optimism on the parts of teachers, parents, and students alike. Don't forget! When we believe we can, we are right.

REFERENCES

American Psychiatric Association (1994) *Diagnostic and Statistical Manual of Mental Disorders (DSM-IV)*. 4th Edition. Washington, DC: American Psychiatric Association.

American Psychiatric Association (2000) "Motor Skill Disorder 315.40." In *Diagnostic and Statistical Manual of Mental Disorders (DSM IV-TR)* (4th Edition, text revision). Washington, DC: American Psychiatric Association.

Amundson, S.J. (1998) *TRICS for Written Communication*. OUT. Kids, Inc. Available at: www.ldonline.org/teaching/focusing_to_learn.html

Attwood, T. (2007) *The Complete Guide to Asperger Syndrome*. London: Jessica Kingsley Publishers.

Barkley, R. (2000) *Taking Charge of AD/HD, Revised Edition: The Complete, Authoritative Guide for Parents*. New York: Guilford Press.

Bregman, A.S. (1994) *Auditory Scene Analysis: The Perceptual Organization of Sound*. Cambridge, MA: The MIT Press.

Cairney, J., Hay, J.A., Faught, B.E. and Hawes, R. (2005) "Developmental coordination disorder and overweight and obesity in children aged 9–14 years." *International Journal of Obesity 29*, 4, 369–372.

Cantell, M. and Kooistra, L. (2002) "Long-term Outcomes of Developmental Coordination Disorder." In S. Cermak and D. Larkin (eds) *Developmental Coordination Disorder* (pp.23–38). New York: Delmar.

Chen, H.F. and Cohn, E.S. (2003) "Social participation for children with developmental coordination disorder: Conceptual, evaluation and intervention considerations." *Physical Occupational Therapy in Pediatrics 23*, 4, 61–78.

Dewey, D., Crawford, S.G., Wilson, B.N. and Kaplan, B.J. (2004) "Co-occurrence of Motor Disorders with Other Childhood Disorders." In D. Dewey and D.E. Tupper (eds) *Developmental Motor Disorders: A Neuropsychological Perspective: The Science and Practice of Neuropsychology* (pp. 405–426). New York: Guilford Press.

Drew, S. (2005) *Developmental Coordination Disorder in Adults*. Chichester, UK: Whurr Publishers Ltd.

Farroni, T., Johnson, M.H., Menon, E., Zulian, L., Faraguna, D. and Csibra, G. (2005) "Newborns' preference for face-relevant stimuli: effects of contrast polarity." *Proceedings of the National Academy of Science 102*, 47, 17245–17250.

Gardner, H. (1999) *Intelligence Reframed: Multiple Intelligences for the 21st Century.* New York: Basic Books.

Gillberg, I.C. and Gillberg, C. (1989) "Asperger syndrome: some epidemiological considerations: a research note." *Journal of Child Psychology and Psychiatry 30*, 631–638.

Golick, M. (1988) *Deal Me In!* Madison, CT: Jeffrey Norton Publishers.

Hallowell, E. (1995) *Driven to Distraction.* New York: Simon and Schuster.

Hellgren, L., Gillberg, I.C., Bagenholm, A. and Gillberg, C. (1994) "Children with deficits in attention, motor control and perception (DAMP) almost grown up: psychiatric and personality disorders at age 16 years." *Journal of Child Psychology and Psychiatry 35*, 255–271.

Kutscher, M.L. (2005) *Kids in the Syndrome Mix of ADHD, LD, Asperger's, Tourette's, Bipolar and More!* London: Jessica Kingsley Publishers.

Learning Disabilities Association of Canada (2002) *Official Definition of Learning Disabilities.* Available at: www.ldac-taac.ca/Defined/defined_new-e.asp

Learning Disabilities Association of Ontario (2001) *Promoting Early Intervention Project.* Available at: www.ldao.ca

Lettvin, J.Y., Maturana, H.R., McCulloch, W.S. and Pitts, W.H. (1959) "What the frog's eye tells the frog's brain." *Proceedings of the Institute of Radio Engineers 47*, 1940–1951.

Losse, A., Henderson, S.E., Elliman, D., Hall, D., Knight, E. and Jongmans, M. (1991) "Clumsiness in children – do they grow out of it? A 10-year follow-up study." *Developmental Medicine and Child Neurology 33*, 55–68.

Lutchmaya, S. and Baron-Cohen, S. (2002) "Human sex differences in social and non-social looking preferences at 12 months." *Infant Behavior and Development 25*, 319–325.

Mamen, M. (1997) *Who's In Charge? A Guide to Family Management.* Carp, Ontario: Creative Bound Inc.

Mamen, M. (1998) *Laughter, Love and Limits: Parenting for Life.* Carp, Ontario: Creative Bound Inc.

Mamen, M. (2006) *The Pampered Child Syndrome: How to Recognize It, How to Manage It and How to Avoid It.* London: Jessica Kingsley Publishers.

Mandich, A.D., Polatajko, H.J., Macnab, J.J. and Miller, L.T. (2001) "Treatment of children with developmental coordination disorder: what is the evidence?" *Physical and Occupational Therapy in Pediatrics 20*, 51–68.

Martini, R., Heath, N. and Missiuna, C. (1999) "A North American analysis of the relationship between learning disabilities and developmental coordination disorder." *International Journal of Special Education 14*, 46–58.

Missiuna, C., Moll, S., Law, M., King, G. and King, S. (2006) "Mysteries and mazes: parent' experiences of developmental coordination disorder." *Canadian Journal of Occupational Therapy 73*, 7–17.

Missiuna, C., Rivard, L. and Bartlett, D. (2003) "Early indentification and risk management of children with developmental coordination disorder." *Pediatric Physical Therapy 15*, 1, 32–38.

Missiuna, C., Rivard, L. and Pollock, N. (2004) "They're bright but can't write: developmental coordination disorder in school aged children." *Teaching Exceptional Children 1* (electronic edition). Available at: www.canchild.ca

Moffitt, A.R. (1971) "Consonant cue perception by twenty to twenty-four week old infants." *Child Development 42*, 717–731.

Molfese, D. (1988) *Brain Lateralization in Children: Developmental Implications.* New York: Guilford Press.

Myers, I.B. and McCaulley, M.H. (1985) *Manual: A Guide to the Development and Use of the Myers-Briggs Type Indicator.* Palo Alto, CA: Consulting Psychologists Press.

Oakland, T., Glutting, J.J. and Horton, C.B. (1996) *Student Styles Questionnaire Manual.* San Antonio: The Psychological Corporation.

Polatajko, H., Fox, M. and Missiuna, C. (1995) "An international consensus on children with developmental coordination disorder." *Canadian Journal of Occupational Therapy 62*, 1, 3–6.

Polatajko, H.J., Mandich, A.D., Miller, L.T. and Macnab, J.J. (2001) "Cognitive orientation to daily occupational performance (CO-OP): Part II – the evidence." *Physical Occupational Therapy in Pediatrics 20*, 2–3, 83–106.

Pollock, N. (2006) *Keeping Current in Sensory Integration.* Hamilton, ON: McMaster University. Available at: www.canchild.ca

Pollock, N. and Missinuna, C. (2005) *To Type or Not to Type…That Is the Question.* Hamilton, ON: McMaster University. Available at www.canchild.ca

Poulsen, A.A. and Ziviani, J.M. (2004) "Can I play too? Physical activity engagement of children with developmental coordination disorders." *Canadian Journal of Occupational Therapy 71*, 2, 100–107.

Rasmussen, P. and Gillberg, C. (2000) "Natural outcome of AD/HD with developmental coordination disorder at age 22 years: a controlled, longitudinal, community-based study." *Journal of the American Academy of Child and Adolescent Psychiatry 39*, 11, 1424–1431.

Rivard, L. and Missiuna, C. (2004) *Encouraging Participation in Physical Activities for Children with Developmental Coordination Disorder.* Hamilton, ON: McMaster University. Available at: www.canchild.ca

Rourke, B. (ed.) (1995) *Syndrome of Nonverbal Learning Disabilities.* New York: Guilford Press.

Rourke, B.P. (1978) "Reading, Spelling, Arithmetic Disabilities: A Neuropsychologic Perspective." In H.R. Myklebust (ed.) *Progress in Learning Disabilities* (Vol. 4, pp.97–120). New York: Grune and Stratton.

Rourke, B.P. and Conway, J.A. (1998) "Disabilities of Arithmetic and Mathematical Reasoning: Perspectives from Neurology and Neuropsychology." In D.P. Rivera (ed.) *Mathematics Education for Students with Learning Disabilities* (pp.59–79). Austin, TX: Pro-Ed.

Sangster, C., Beninger, C., Polatajko, H.J. and Mandich, A. (2005) "Cognitive strategy generation in children with developmental coordination disorder." *Canadian Journal of Occupational Therapy 72*, 2, 67–77.

Schnurr, R. (1999) *Asperger's, Huh! A Child's Perspective.* Ottawa, Ontario: Anisor Publishing.

Skinner, R.A. and Piek, J.P. (2001) "Psychosocial implications of poor motor coordination in children and adolescents." *Human Movement Science 20*, 1–2, 73–94.

Stewart, K. (2002) *Helping a Child with Nonverbal Learning Disorder or Asperger's Syndrome.* Oakland, CA: New Harbinger Publications.

Swihart, E.W. and Cotter, P. (1998) *The Manipulative Child: How to Regain Control and Raise Resilient, Resourceful, and Independent Kids.* New York: MacMillan.

Szatmari, P. (1992) "A review of the DSM-III-R criteria for autistic disorder." *Journal of Autism and Developmental Disorders 22*, 507–523.

Thompson, S. (1997) *The Source for Nonverbal Learning Disabilities.* East Moline, IL: Linguisystems.

Visser, J. (2003) "Developmental coordination disorder: A review of research on subtypes and comorbidities." *Human Movement Science 22*, 4–5, 479–493.

Wilson, P.H. (2005) "Practitioner review: approaches to assessment and treatment of children with DCD: an evaluative review." *Journal of Child Psychology and Psychiatry 46*, 8, 806–823.

World Health Organization (1993) *The ICD-10 Classification of Mental and Behavioral Disorders: Diagnostic Criteria for Research.* Geneva: WHO.

RESOURCES

Useful websites

abcteach – www.abcteach.com
This is an extremely practical, award-winning, "hands-on" website providing actual downloadable worksheets and other resources for a wide range of learning needs.

CanChild Centre for Childhood Disability Research – www.canchild.ca
Unlike others in this list, this website from McMaster University in Hamilton, Ontario, is specifically for those interested in cutting-edge research on childhood disabilities.

CHADD (Children and Adults with Attention Deficit/Hyperactivity Disorder) – www.chadd.org
Founded in 1987, this website was originally created "in response to the frustration and sense of isolation experienced by parents and their children with AD/HD."

Internet Mental Health – www.mentalhealth.com
This U.S. based website provides a thorough overview, and resources list, for a wide range of mental health disorders, including Asperger's and AD/HD.

LD Online – www.ldonline.org
Claiming to be "the world's leading website on learning disabilities and ADHD," this site includes links to easy-to-understand articles and resources for parents, educators, and other professionals.

Learning Disabilities Association of Canada – www.ldac-taac.ca
The website of the Learning Disabilities Association of Canada (Troubles d'apprentissage – Association canadienne) provides bilingual resource information on a wide range of learning disabilities and includes a resource centre.

Learning Disabilities Association of Ontario – www.ldao.ca
Although not specific to NLD, the user-friendly website of the Learning Disabilities
Association of Ontario provides information and links to a wide range of resources,
including a web-based teaching tool for educators.

Medline – www.medline.com
This website is specifically for members of the medical profession who can access
information with respect to a full range of disorders that fall within the medical scope of
practice, including Developmental Coordination Disorder and AD/HD.

National Institute of Mental Health – www.nimh.nih.gov/publicat/ADHD.cfm
A thorough overview of AD/HD from the National Institute of Mental Health addresses
issues such as differential diagnosis, possible causality, and various interventions.

NLDline – www.nldline.com
This is a popular, informative, accessible, and supportive website geared to increasing
awareness of NLD among parents and professionals.

NLD on the Web – www.nldontheweb.org
A broad-based and thorough overview of NLD is provided on this neuropsychologically
oriented site, including an exhaustive list of professional references.

Nonverbal Learning Disorders Association – www.nlda.org
The official website of the Nonverbal Learning Disorders Association reflects the
organization's dedication to research, education, and advocacy for nonverbal learning
disorders.

WordQTM Writing Software – www.wordq.com
This is a commercial website for writing software, included here as an example of
resources available on the open market for individuals with written expressive difficulties.

ABOUT THE AUTHOR

Dr. Maggie Mamen is a psychologist in a multidisciplinary private practice in Ontario, Canada. She has been employed in university, hospital and school board settings, and has been interested in learning disabilities, particularly in girls, for over 25 years. Maggie gives many presentations to parents, professionals, and community groups nationally and internationally, and has been acknowledged by the Ontario Psychological Association for her outstanding contribution to mental health in education. In addition to her clinical work with children, adolescents, and families, she is the author of three books: *Who's In Charge? A Guide to Family Management* (Creative Bound, 1997); *Laughter, Love and Limits: Parenting for Life* (Creative Bound, 1998); and *The Pampered Child Syndrome: How to Recognize It, How to Manage It and How to Avoid It* (Jessica Kingsley Publishers, 2006). The mother of three now-adult children and grandmother of one, she lives with her husband on the edge of the countryside in Ottawa.

SUBJECT INDEX

Note: Abbreviations used: non-verbal learning disorder: NLD; learning disorder: LD; Asperger's Syndrome: AS; Attention Deficit Hyperactivity Disorder: ADHD

AUTHOR INDEX

American Psychiatric Association 33, 78, 94
Amundson, S.J. 151
Attwood, T. 128

Barkley, R. 154
Baron-Cohen, S. 53
Bartlett, D. 94
Bregman, A.S. 48

Cairney, J. 95
Cantell, M. 95
Chen, H.F. 95
Cohn, E.S. 95
Cotter, P. 154

Dewey, D. 95
Drew, S. 95

Farroni, T. 52
Fox, M. 94

Gardner, H. 37
Gillberg, C. 78–9, 95
Gillberg, I.C. 78–9
Glutting, J.J. 73, 82
Golick, M. 122, 145

Hallowell, E. 154
Heath, N. 97
Hellgren, L. 95
Horton, C.B. 73, 82

Kooistra, L. 95
Kutscher, M.L. 33

Learning Disabilities Association of Canada 11
Learning Disabilities Association of Ontario 11
Lettvin, J.Y. 47
Losse, A. 95
Lutchmaya, S. 53

Mamen, M. 94, 160
Mandich, A.D. 138
Martini, R. 97
McCaulley, M.H. 73, 110

Missiuna, C. 94, 96, 97, 138
Moffitt, A.R. 49
Molfese, D. 57
Myers, I.B. 73, 110

Oakland, T. 73, 82, 110

Piek, J.P. 95
Polatajko, H. 94, 138
Pollock, N. 96, 138
Poulsen, A.A. 95

Rasmussen, P. 95
Rivard, L. 94, 96, 138
Rourke, B. 20, 63, 101

Sangster, C. 138
Schnurr, R. 80
Skinner, R.A. 95
Stewart, K. 77, 128
Swihart, E.W. 153
Szatmari, P. 78–9

Thompson, S. 20

Visser, J. 94

Wilson, P.H. 138
World Health Organization 78

Ziviani, J.M. 95